LYING IN WAIT

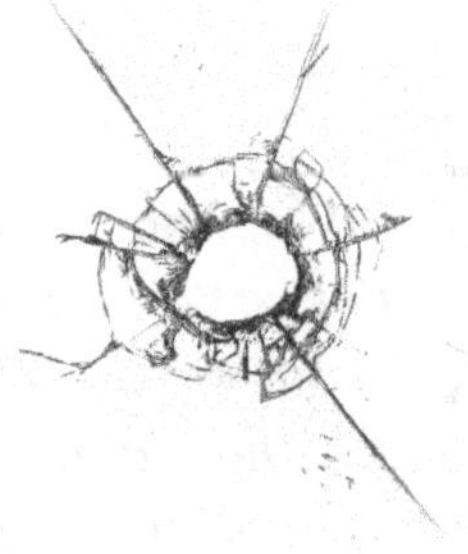

ANATOMY OF A DOMESTIC TERRORIST

HOWARD FRANK

WILD BLUE PRESS

WildBluePress.com

LYING
IN WAIT

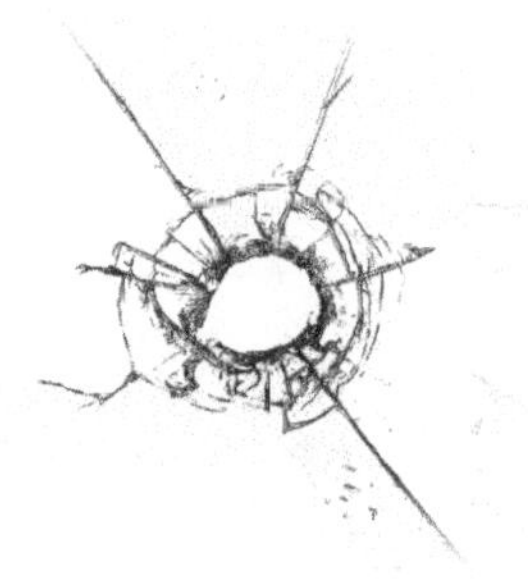

CONTENTS

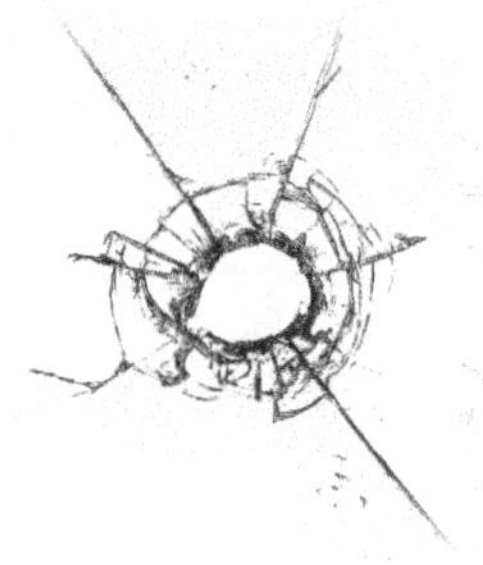

THE AMBUSH

UNQUIET SLUMBERS

In the northeastern corner of Pennsylvania, the Pocono Mountains roll toward the Delaware River in undulating waves of granite and shale. The town of Blooming Grove drowses among stands of oak, maple, and pine that have watched over this landscape since before the first European settlers arrived. It is a place where wilderness still presses close against civilization, where state game lands stretch for thousands of acres in every direction, and where a man might disappear into the forest and not be seen again for months, if ever.

The upcoming autumn of 2014 had painted these mountains in their early seasonal disguise of gold and crimson, a pastoral deception that would soon harbor one of the most ruthless acts of calculated violence the Commonwealth of Pennsylvania had witnessed in years. The story begins not with the crack of rifle fire that would shatter the evening quiet of September 12, but rather, in the months, perhaps years, of methodical preparation that preceded it, in the twisted psychology of a man whose hatred had crystallized into something approaching art, if art can be said to encompass the precise choreography of murder.

Eric Matthew Frein was 31 when he began his final preparations, transforming himself with the ritualistic precision of a warrior preparing for battle. He was a lean man of medium height—about 5 feet 7 inches tall and 160 pounds—with dark brown hair that he shaved on both sides in a modified Mohawk, a radical departure from the short, neatly groomed hairstyle he had worn for years.

His pale complexion and sharp, angular features gave him an intense appearance that those who knew him would later describe as unsettling, particularly when combined with the cold calculation that marked his final months of preparation.

What authorities would later describe as "mental preparation to commit this cowardly act," this physical transformation was the external manifestation of an internal metamorphosis—the visible sign that Eric Frein was no longer merely Eric Frein but something else entirely: an instrument of vengeance against what he perceived as a corrupt system.

The Pennsylvania State Police barracks in Blooming Grove Township was an unremarkable building, utilitarian in the way of all government structures, situated in a wooded area and surrounded by state game lands. But to Frein's calculating mind, it represented the perfect convergence of symbolism and tactical opportunity, a facility isolated enough to provide escape routes but significant enough to send the message he intended to deliver.

On the morning of September 12, 2014, Frein moved through his pre-attack routine with the methodical precision of a man who had rehearsed every detail. Hours before his unforeseen act of violence, he sent a text message to a friend: **All is good** and **I stayed at your place last night**, casual words that masked the enormity of what he was planning. These would be among the last normal communications Eric Frein would send as a free man.

As evening approached, Frein gathered his equipment: a .308-caliber rifle with scope, carefully zeroed for the distance he had measured between his chosen firing position and the barracks entrance. He had selected his position with the eye of a professional sniper, finding a spot in the treeline that provided both concealment and a clear field of fire. The shooting position was marked by two trees rising from the forest floor, forming a "V," each trunk later slashed with orange spray paint by investigators, 82 yards from the front door of the barracks—just enough space between the trees to provide a clear shot.

A .308-caliber rifle, when cradled in the hands of a practiced marksman, is an instrument of singular and chilling authority. The cartridge itself—a short, bottlenecked vessel of brass and lead—has been engineered for a kind of efficiency that borders on the ruthless. At the moment of firing, the bullet, often weighing 150 to 180 grains, is propelled from the muzzle at velocities approaching 2,800 feet per second, its energy at that instant measured not in abstract numbers, but in certainty and consequence.

That is nearly 2.5 times the speed of sound, and faster than the top speed of an F-16.

The .308's reputation is not born of rumor, but of results. At distances up to a thousand yards, it retains the power to punch through bone, muscle, even the armored vests sometimes worn by those who expect and prepare for violence. Hunters favor it for elk and deer, lawmen for its accuracy and the grim reliability with which it delivers its verdict. The recoil is manageable, almost civilized, but the wound it inflicts is devastating.

Sometime before 11:00 p.m. on the night of September 12, Frein "slithered" into the brush, as prosecutors would later describe it, set up his rifle and scope, and took aim at the doorway to the barracks. There, in the gathering darkness, he settled into the patient stillness that his years of hunting and military simulation had taught him. The barracks parking lot was illuminated by security lights, creating a stage-like setting where the evening's drama would unfold.

At approximately 10:50 p.m., during the ritual of shift change that marked the transition from day to night patrol, Corporal Bryon K. Dickson II stepped into the parking lot. To understand the magnitude of what was lost in that moment, one must understand the man himself, a figure who embodied the quiet heroism that defines the best of American law enforcement.

Dickson was 38 years old, a stockily built man of medium height whose presence commanded respect without demanding it. His dark hair was kept in the regulation style that marked career law enforcement officers, while his steady brown eyes reflected the kind of thoughtful intelligence that had made him a natural leader among his peers. There was about him the bearing of a man who had served in two uniforms with equal distinction, first as a Marine, where he had learned the discipline that would define his approach to law enforcement, and later as a Pennsylvania State Police trooper who took seriously the motto inscribed on every department vehicle: "Honor, Service, Integrity."

After graduating from the Pennsylvania State Police Academy in Hershey in 2007, he had been stationed in Hazleton and near Philadelphia for most of his seven-year career as a state trooper, building a reputation for professionalism and dedication that marked him as one of the department's rising stars.

But statistics and career highlights cannot capture the human dimension of Bryon Dickson. He was a husband to a wife who worked as a nurse, dedicating her life to caring for others with the same spirit of service that had drawn her husband to law enforcement. He was the father of two young sons who would now grow up with only photographs and stories to remember the man who had read them bedtime stories and taught them to throw a baseball. His funeral, held at St. Peter's Cathedral in Scranton, drew thousands of mourners, a testament to the impact one man can have when he lives his life in service to others.

Standing nearby Dickson that fateful night was Trooper Alex Douglass, 27 years old and representing a new generation of Pennsylvania State Police officers. Douglass was a tall, athletic man whose lean frame reflected the dedication to physical fitness that had made him an accomplished ultramarathon runner. His light brown hair was cropped short in the military style favored by many state troopers, while his blue eyes held the kind of determined focus that had carried him through 50-mile races and would later sustain him through months of painful rehabilitation. There was about him the quiet confidence of a man who had pushed his body to its limits and found that those limits were farther than most people ever imagined.

Douglass had followed a path that exemplified the American dream: the son of working-class parents, he had earned his way to the University of Scranton, where he studied finance and economics from 2001 to 2005. The dedication that would later help him survive Frein's bullet was evident even then. He graduated on a Friday and reported to the state police academy the following Sunday, eager to begin his career in public service.

Douglass brought to law enforcement the same drive that had made him an accomplished athlete. His nightly phone call to his girlfriend, a ritual that had become their way of maintaining connection despite the demands of shift work, would be interrupted by gunfire, setting in motion a medical odyssey that would test every ounce of that hard-earned resilience.

Douglass was on the phone with his girlfriend for his nightly reassurance that he had arrived safely at the Blooming Grove barracks for his 11:00 p.m. shift. It was the kind of small domestic detail that takes on enormous significance in retrospect, a reminder that behind every badge is a human being with relationships, responsibilities, and dreams that extend far beyond the uniform.

The night held its breath. Up in the dark like a patient sentry, Frein remained motionless, a shadow among shadows, the forest drawn close around him like a conspirator. The hour was late enough that the air had cooled, but not enough to bite, and the only movement was the occasional tremble of a leaf—small, uncertain, when a faint wind tested its hold.

Through the glass of his scope, he studied the figure below. Corporal Bryon Dickson was unaware of the story he now occupied, a character stepping unsuspectingly into the hinge of an unfolding tragedy. His walk was neither hurried nor slow, just the even cadence of an ordinary night, the rhythm of a man certain of tomorrow.

Frein's cheek lay against the rifle stock, his breathing measured, his mind narrowed to the tunnel between reticle and target. In this sliver of time, nothing else existed; not his past, not his escape, only the mechanics of what must be done. The forest, the parking lot, the man, all were reduced to shapes, distances, and inevitabilities.

One finger curled inward, the pad of it resting on steel, pressure building with a patient certainty. And then, without drama, without warning, metal snapped forward, fire bloomed in the chamber, and sound broke the still night like a pane of glass struck from within. In that instant, the world tipped: Dickson's body crumpled toward the earth, and somewhere out in the sleeping county, the first invisible threads of a manhunt began to draw tight.

The clinical and haunting way a high-powered rifle round such as the .308 enters and devastates the human body is a cruel journey.

It happens in an instant, so swiftly it rarely admits comprehension: the trigger's crisp break, the brief, silent surge of recoil, and already the bullet, a copper-jacketed thing no longer than a cigarette filter, travels faster than thought toward its recipient. When it arrives, it does not so much pierce as declare its authority. The entrance is narrow, deceptively modest. Yet beyond that portal lies calamity.

What the eye cannot follow, the body feels: pressure rising, tissue surrendering, bone reduced to a fragile architecture no sturdier than spun glass. The bullet spins as it drives forward, carving not a single track but a whirlwind path, generating a cavity that balloons out and collapses in the same breath. In that moment, an orderly anatomy, the careful arrangement of vessels and organs, disintegrates.

And all of it seems, to the witness, eerily silent; there is no cry exact enough, no word sufficiently sharp to match the shock of the devastation. Afterward, one is left only with the small, round entrance wound, hardly more than a blemish, and, depending on the bullet's persistence, a jagged, ruinous exit on the far side. The contrast—modest beginning, extravagant conclusion—bares the precise cruelty of fact.

The first shot found Dickson with the precision that Frein had spent months perfecting. The .308-caliber bullet struck him in the chest, killing him instantly. His life ended without warning in the harsh glare of the parking lot lights, without the chance to draw his weapon or take cover. Death arrived with the clinical efficiency that Frein had rehearsed in his mind countless times.

Douglass, hearing what he would later describe as a loud crack, cut short his phone conversation.

"I gotta go. I'll call you back," he told his girlfriend, not knowing that these might be the last coherent words she would hear him speak for months. Moving instinctively to help his fallen colleague, Douglass had barely taken a step when the second shot found him. The bullet tore through the left side of his back, punching through his right hip and pelvis, leaving what he would later testify was a wound "probably the size of a silver dollar."

The projectile's path through Douglass's body was devastating. It shattered bones, severed nerves, and left him partially paralyzed, his right leg essentially destroyed. He fell to the pavement beside his dead colleague, his body going into shock as blood pooled beneath him in the late summer night. His fellow troopers, arriving at the scene moments later, performed emergency first aid before he was airlifted to Geisinger Medical Center, where he was classified as being in stable but critical condition, medical euphemisms that barely conveyed the magnitude of his injuries.

What followed for Alex Douglass was a medical odyssey that would span years and test the limits of human endurance. In the first 30 days alone, he underwent 11 surgeries as doctors fought to save his life and what remained of his mobility. Over the following months and years, that number would climb to 16 major operations, each one attempting to repair the catastrophic damage that Frein's bullet had inflicted. Surgeons worked to reconstruct his shattered pelvis, to repair nerve damage, to salvage what they could of his right leg.

But the human body has its limits, and even the most skilled medical intervention could not undo the precision of Frein's marksmanship. In December 2018, more than four years after the shooting, Douglass made the agonizing decision to have his right leg amputated below the knee, the consequence of blood vessel damage that the dispassionate bullet wreaked on the intricate blood supplies to his lower extremity. It became the final acknowledgment that some wounds are beyond healing. The man who had once completed a 50-mile ultramarathon would spend the rest of his life learning to walk again with an artificial hip and a prosthetic leg, permanent reminders of that September night when hatred masqueraded as patriotism.

In those few seconds, Eric Frein had achieved what he had likely dreamed of for months: he had struck at the heart of what he perceived as an oppressive system, leaving one man dead and another permanently maimed.

He then disappeared into the night.

Driving with his lights off on Pennsylvania Route 402, Frein apparently failed to see a T-junction, lost control of his 2001 Jeep Cherokee, and drove into a swamp. Authorities speculated that he then traveled 15 to 20 miles on foot to Canadensis, Pennsylvania, where his parents lived. Three days later, investigators would find the abandoned vehicle and, inside it, what amounted to Frein's calling card: bullet casings that matched those from the crime scene, a cache of evidence so obviously incriminating that one might wonder if some unconscious part of the killer wanted to be caught.

But Frein himself had vanished into the 300 square miles of dense Pennsylvania woodland that surrounded his parents' home, terrain he knew as intimately as other men knew their neighborhood streets. Here, in the realm of his expertise, he transformed from amateur terrorist to quarry in what would become one of the most expensive and extensive manhunts in Pennsylvania history.

AN ORDINARY NIGHT

The hour is late, nearing the 11:00 changeover, and the Blooming Grove barracks sits isolated in the deep Pennsylvania dark, a utilitarian island of brick and fluorescent light. Inside, the atmosphere is sedative, the routine utterly regular. Christine Donahue, a police communications operator who has known this rhythm for three and a half years, is finishing her shift, preparing for the arrival of her relief, Nicole Palmer.

Corporal Bryon K. Dickson II, a man of solid build and unsuspecting future, steps into the light. He exchanges a pleasantry, a quick, vanishing joke with Palmer, and then disappears into the Corporals' Office. Donahue moves with the dull comfort of habit, gathering the day's Incident Memos to distribute to the mailboxes in the Patrol Room. She stands there now among the inter-office slots, flanked by the gray uniforms of Trooper William Fells, Trooper Benjamin Jones, and Trooper Randal Troaini.

Then, the silence of the woods is ruptured. Three loud bangs—sharp, flat, intrusive. For a heartbeat, there is no terror, only a suspended confusion. The men in uniform merely look at one another, a silent communion of "What was that?"

Donahue returns to her glass cage, the Communications Room. On the other side, in the exposed lobby, Nicole Palmer is frantic, her palms hammering against the safety glass. The words are a scream.

"Christine, let me in! Dickson has been shot. Let me in!"

Donahue hits the release, and the horror enters the room.

Outside, in the cold air, Palmer had seen the mechanics of death up close. She had rushed out after the first shots, only to hear the crack of a second shot and witness a small, terrifying phenomenon: a "perfect circle of dust" settling at her foot, the quiet proof of a bullet meant for her.

Nearby, Corporal Dickson lay on the pavement, his face drained of color, lips mouthing a final, desperate plea to the empty night. "Help me."

From her desk, Donahue witnesses the second act. Trooper Alex Douglass approaches the entrance, a silhouette against the night. Another report echoes, a single bang, and Douglass collapses, folded by unseen mechanics to the floor. Unable to reach 911, Donahue retreats, fumbling to dial the non-emergency line for ambulances, before rushing back to the Patrol Room to deliver the impossible news to the startled men: "We have two troopers that have been shot!"

In the Patrol Room, the television flickers. Trooper William Fells, a Marine with 12 years of road behind him, and his pupil, Benjamin Jones, fresh from the academy and the sands of Iraq, are finishing the paperwork of a quiet shift. Fells had heard the sound—like a round fired at the range—but the mind rejects the impossible; he dismissed it, assuming something had merely been dropped.

The brittle calm shatters when Palmer bursts in. "Guys, Dickson has been shot." Fells is shocked, his mind grasping for a rational explanation—a traffic stop gone wrong, perhaps. But then Palmer returns with the grim amendment. "Douglass is shot in the legs."

Fells looks through the window. He sees Douglass propped on his elbows, a broken figure on the lobby linoleum. The front door glass is busted out, a jagged mouth. Beyond it, lying on the pavement under the pitiless security lights, is the uniformed body of Corporal Dickson.

Instinct takes over. Fells assumes command. He organizes the men—Jones, Troaini, Scochin—ordering them to retrieve long guns. With Jones covering him with an AR-15, Fells moves into the hallway to the wounded Douglass.

"I can't move," Douglass says, whispering the geography of his attacker. "The woods across the street."

Fells runs downstairs, alerting the arriving midnight shift—Trooper Yanochko among them—to gear up. A plan is struck, desperate and improvised: use an SUV as a shield. Fells drives, reversing the vehicle between the fallen corporal and the black, treelined void across the road. He leaps out. He yells for Troopers Seymour and Golden. In a swift, frantic maneuver, they grasp Corporal Dickson, dragging the dead weight of their brother across the asphalt and into the lobby. Fells, mindful of the invisible eye watching them, grabs the fallen firearms from the pavement and moves the SUV to the lower level, denying the attacker any cover.

Trooper Jones, who had stared down the chaos, now packs the wound in Douglass's hip. Nearby, on the floor, the rituals of survival are performed on the unresponsive Dickson—CPR, the defibrillator—but the machine offers no rhythm, no pulse.

Trooper Robert Golden, a sergeant in the Marine Corps trained in the dark arts of the counter-sniper, understands the trap immediately. He knows the tactic: shoot one to create bait, then kill the rescuers. He was changing in the locker room when the news came, and his first thought was of blood—that Dickson would bleed out. He moves with the extraction team, shielding himself, dragging the body.

Once inside, Golden moves through the building, extinguishing lights, drawing blinds, plunging the barracks into darkness to blind the sniper watching from the road. He checks on Douglass, then joins the futile effort to revive Dickson. Trooper Yanochko, clutching a shotgun, helps hold the door as the body is dragged inside. The men work in the dark, the ordinary night having been replaced by a sudden, violent siege.

THE MECHANICS OF DEATH

The Barracks' surveillance system acts as a stuttering, indifferent witness, blind to the fluidity of time. It does not capture the stream of life but only its static interruptions, a series of frozen pictures cycled every second, a mechanical blink that misses the violence even as it records the result.

On this one-second interval, the brutal velocity of the attack is laid bare. Corporal Dickson, the man who only moments ago had traded a pleasantry, steps through the front doors. In one frame, he is upright, a figure of authority; in the next, he has been erased from the vertical world, collapsed almost immediately onto the sidewalk. There is no stumble, no gradual surrender—only the sudden, terrible gravity of the dead.

Inside, on the small, glowing square of the surveillance monitor, PCO Palmer watches the nightmare unfold in these jerky, halting frames. Trooper Douglass appears, a silhouette of rescue, only to be folded by the unseen force. He collapses, and the screen captures the grim pantomime of his survival: a frame of him falling, a frame of him dragging his body across the lobby floor, the wake of the fourth shot trailing him.

Outside, the camera holds its steady, unblinking gaze on the murdered corporal, now motionless on the pavement, a final, static portrait of a man lying there with blood spilling from his mouth.

And what the camera cannot see, the laws of physics demand. The bullet, that copper-jacketed agent of the end, does not merely pierce; it devastates. It spins as it drives forward, carving not a single track but a whirlwind path, a miniature cyclone of destruction that generates a cavity ballooning out and collapsing in the same breath. In that split second, the careful, miraculous arrangement of vessels and organs simply disintegrates. Afterward, the body is left with the deception of the wound: a small, round entrance masking the jagged, ruinous exit on the far side where life has rushed out.

THE IMPOSITION OF ORDER

Chaos demands a center of gravity, and William Fells, a Trooper First Class with the discipline of the Marine Corps stamped into his spine, provides it.

He instantly takes command.

He orders the remaining men to retrieve "weapons and shields," transforming the raw terror of the barracks into a practiced, desperate military action. He and Trooper Benjamin Jones perform the grim duty of dragging the wounded Douglass back inside, a final, necessary task before the evacuation.

Then come the cold architects of the state's certainty— Robert Golden, Gregory Yanochko, Brian Seymour, Michael Miller, Michael Cummings, Sabrina Gumble, Sean Doran, and George Murphy.

These are the analysts and technicians who descend upon the aftermath. They are called to fill the vacuum of shock with unassailable fact, mapping the location of every casing, every bullet fragment, and the precise geometry of the crime scene. Among them, James Hitchcock moves as the central figure carrying the ballistic truth—the final, absolute evidence that will eventually close the distance between the trauma of the night and the calculating mind of the hunter in the woods.

The emotional weight of the scene tests the limits of composure for everyone present.

As the reality of Corporal Dickson's final moments settles into the room, the men and women of the barracks are visibly affected. Some surely must look away, unable to maintain eye contact with the destruction of their own sanctuary, while others stare down at their tasks, their faces set in grave expressions.

The weight of their responsibility—to determine exactly how this happened—is heavy in the air.

They maintain the professional demeanor the investigation requires, cataloging the horror with careful attention to every detail. But the subtle signs of the toll are there: the pause in activity during a particularly graphic discovery, the collective intake of breath when the full scope of the violence is realized, and the careful way they move around the evidence of a man who, just moments ago, was one of them.

THE SEA OF GRAY

The funeral of a state trooper is a piece of theater designed to impose order on the chaos of death. It is a spectacle of geometry and silence. In Scranton, under a sky the color of a bruised plum, the "Sea of Gray" assembled, with thousands of troopers from across the continent standing in rigid, unwavering lines. They were a wall of slate wool and polished leather, a collective refusal to accept the randomness of the violence that had brought them there.

But strip away the pageantry—the bagpipes keening their high, desperate notes, the flag folded with the sharp precision of origami—and one is left with the ghost of a man who was, until very recently, concerned with much smaller things.

Bryon Dickson was not born a martyr. He was a man who built things. In the garage of his home, amid the smell of sawdust and engine oil, unfinished projects now sat gathering the quiet dust of the sudden departure. There was a workbench where he had taught his sons the value of a straight line and a measured cut. He was a Marine before he was a trooper, a man who had traded the expansive dangers of foreign soil for the deceptive safety of the Pennsylvania roads, believing, perhaps, that he had found a place where the rules were clear and the risks calculated.

He was the "scrappy" one, the trooper who did not just wear the uniform but inhabited it with a kinetic energy that his fellow officers respected.

But it is in the absences that the ghost is most palpable. It is in the empty chair at the dinner table, a void that sucks the air out of the room. It is in the baseball practice where a father should be leaning against a chain-link fence, shouting encouragement, but is instead represented only by a memory that is already beginning to stiffen into legend.

His reputation among the men was not one of reckless heroism, but of reliable solidity. He was the backup one hoped for when the radio crackled with bad news. Now, that reliability had been converted into a symbol. To the public, he was Corporal Dickson, the fallen hero. To his wife, watching the flag pass from a gloved hand to her own, he was the warmth that had vanished from the other side of the bed, the silence in the house that no amount of bagpipe music could ever fill.

THE HUNT

NEEDLE IN A HAYSTACK

The human element of the search was equally impressive. Teams of officers, many of them volunteers from departments across Pennsylvania and neighboring states, combed through abandoned buildings, searched caves and rocky outcroppings, and followed every lead, no matter how tenuous. The phrase that came to define their methodology was "grid searches, woodland searches, house-to-house, cabin-to-cabin," a comprehensive approach that left nothing to chance. Every structure within the search area was methodically examined, from occupied homes to forgotten hunting cabins, from active businesses to long-abandoned industrial sites.

Psychological warfare played its own role in the operation. Authorities deliberately publicized their methods, hoping to convince Frein that escape was impossible. They spoke openly about their thermal imaging capabilities, their tracking dogs, their growing database of evidence. The message was clear: we know who you are, we know where you have been, and we will find you. It was a calculated attempt to erode the morale of a man who had counted on his survivalist skills to keep him free indefinitely.

The coordination required for such a massive operation was extraordinary. Multiple jurisdictions, each with their own procedures and command structures, had to work together seamlessly. Communication protocols were established to prevent the kind of friendly-fire incidents that could occur when several heavily armed teams operated in the same area. Helicopter flights were coordinated with ground operations to prevent accidents. Supply lines were established to keep search teams fed, armed, and equipped during extended operations in remote areas.

Intelligence gathering became a crucial component of the search. Authorities analyzed Frein's computer searches, which revealed that he had researched "placing supply caches, police manhunt techniques and how to evade them" going back to 2012. This intelligence painted a picture of a man who had spent years preparing for exactly this scenario, studying law enforcement tactics with the dedication of a military strategist. It also revealed the scope of his planning—this was not a crime of passion but a calculated act of terrorism that had been years in the making.

While Lieutenant Colonel George Bivens commanded the cameras and the public imagination, District Attorney Ray Tonkin commanded the paper trail that fueled the machine. In the cramped, coffee-fueled confines of the Pike County DA's office, lights burned through the night as Tonkin acted as the silent architect of the siege. A former municipal police officer who carried his frame with the tension of a coiled spring, Tonkin knew that catching Frein was only half the battle; keeping him caught was the other.

He understood that a defense attorney would one day pick apart this manhunt with the luxury of hindsight, looking for a single procedural error to set a cop killer free. Every warrant for a cabin search, every wiretap on a family member, and every deployment of surveillance tech had to pass across Tonkin's desk for legal triage. He was building the cage long before the animal was captured, operating under the crushing weight of a community looking to him for a resolution that bullets alone could not provide.

The technology deployed against a single man hiding in the woods was staggering in its sophistication. Helicopters equipped with thermal imaging equipment swept the canopy day and night, their rotors beating a constant rhythm over the treetops as they searched for the heat signature of a human form among the leaves. The thermal imaging cameras could detect temperature differences as small as a few degrees, capable of spotting a man-sized heat source even through dense forest cover. Night vision equipment allowed search teams to continue their work in darkness, turning the 24-hour cycle into one continuous hunt.

Search dogs trained to track human scent worked the woodland trails, their handlers moving through the underbrush with the methodical precision of a military operation, following scent trails that often led to nothing but empty forest and the maddening sense that their quarry had been watching them all along. German shepherds and Belgian Malinois, chosen for their stamina and tracking ability, could follow a human scent trail for miles through difficult terrain, but Frein's knowledge of counter-tracking techniques—gleaned from his online research into police manhunt methods—allowed him to evade even these sophisticated biological sensors.

Perhaps most remarkably, authorities deployed what they called a "blimp in a box," a $180,000 tethered helium balloon equipped with surveillance cameras, borrowed from the Ohio Department of Transportation. This experimental contraption hovered above the search area like some mechanical vulture, its electronic eyes scanning the forest floor for any sign of movement. The balloon could remain aloft for days at a time, providing continuous surveillance of key areas while freeing helicopters for more dynamic search patterns. It was technology bordering on science fiction, deployed against a man whose greatest weapons were his knowledge of the terrain and his ability to remain motionless for hours at a time.

It was not a thing of beauty. If asked, a layman would likely call it a trailer, or perhaps a large, aluminum shed on wheels. Its exterior was a dull, non-committal color, a shade one might find on an institutional wall or the hull of a military transport. It sat upon the asphalt with a perfect stillness, unadorned and without pretense, a stark block of modern utility in the sprawling, forested expanse of the Poconos.

Yet this unremarkable box, so plain in its outward bearing, contained within it a most curious thing. It was a balloon, a bladder of impermeable fabric, waiting for a breath of gas. When the mechanism was activated with a low, hydraulic hiss and the measured rush of helium, the side of the box would lower itself like the drawbridge of a miniature fortress, and the thing would emerge. A blimp, yes, but of a different sort than those great, ponderous airships of a forgotten age. This was a tethered beast, a creature of duty and of purpose.

Once it had ascended, pulled by its own helium-borne buoyancy, the thing would hang in the air at a height of several hundred feet, a silent sentry with a single, unblinking eye of glass. The eye, a camera of exceptional clarity and power, was capable of discerning the form of a man from three miles away, a moving vehicle from five. It did not blink, did not tire, did not grow cold. Its gaze was as relentless and detached as the blue sky itself.

A single taut umbilical cord of wire and fiber optics kept it moored to the ground, feeding it power and carrying back the images it collected—a continuous stream of silent, dispassionate observation. It was a witness to all things below: the fleeting, furtive movements of a prison yard, the slow, tectonic shifts of a highway construction site, the pulsing, faceless crowds at a public fair. This was its purpose, its unalterable function. It was a thing of constant vigil, a mechanical observer brought into being to ensure that no one, anywhere, would be entirely alone.

Armored BearCat vehicles patrolled the forest roads, their bulletproof hulls and gunports a testament to the deadly nature of their quarry. These mine-resistant vehicles, originally designed for urban warfare, proved surprisingly effective in the wooded terrain, able to transport tactical teams quickly to areas where Frein had been spotted while providing protection against sniper fire. The sight of these military-grade vehicles rolling through the pastoral Pocono countryside served as a constant reminder that a war was being fought in America's back yard.

The BearCat is hulking yet deliberate, built high on the chassis of a Ford Super Duty truck. Its flanks bristle with plated steel and bulletproof glass—no nonsense, no flare. In the autumn haze, it crept along backwoods roads, tires shouldering aside shale and broken branches, its silhouette simultaneously reassuring and faintly ominous. If a small town dreads the unknown, so too does it yearn for rescue, muscled into the form of this mechanical beast.

Inside, the BearCat's heart is utilitarian: a blast-resistant floor, .50-caliber bulletproof windows, an open plan for up to a dozen men kitted in fear and discipline. The seats are not comfortable, but they are aligned for purpose: to carry the living and, if fate twists cruel, to retrieve the fallen. There are ports for rifles, a hatch atop for the wary head of a marksman or negotiator, places to mount battering rams and breathe bottled air if the world outside fills with gas or flames. It moves with a surprising agility for a thing so heavy, able to turn in tight corners and ford the bruised streams and mud slicks of the wild. Its armor is not theatrical but practical: military-grade steel meant to deflect not the fantasy of destruction, but the real heat of rifle fire.

And so, during the search—when helicopters scrawled dark signatures in the sky and patrols swept through shivering timber—the BearCat pressed on through the panic and the press of onlookers. It was a fortress with wheels, a symbol of resolve in a landscape that had forgotten its safety. To the officers, each movement through the countryside became a confession and a prayer; they trusted the BearCat to shield them from the very evil they meant to confront.

If Frein watched from the woods, as no doubt he did, the sight of the BearCat, indifferent to gunfire, slow and certain, must have confirmed what all fugitives eventually learn: no matter how deep the forest, death and justice would arrive wrapped in steel, unhurried and unafraid.

The sightings of Frein that punctuated the manhunt demonstrated both the effectiveness and the limitations of the search operation. On multiple occasions, officers came tantalizingly close to their quarry. At one point, tracking dogs flushed him from a hiding spot, but darkness allowed him to escape deeper into the woods. These near-misses generated their own tactical responses: helicopters would converge, their spotlights sweeping the forest floor in brilliant white columns, search teams would race to establish a perimeter, and the surrounding area would be locked down as officers moved through the woods with the caution of soldiers entering hostile territory.

The psychological toll on the search teams was considerable. Day after day, they trudged through difficult terrain, following leads that led nowhere, searching buildings that had been searched previously, maintaining the kind of vigilance that Frein's reputation as a skilled marksman demanded. The knowledge that their quarry was armed with a high-powered rifle and had already killed one of their own added an element of personal danger to every step they took in the wilderness.

The region became what one journalist called "the Frein Zone," a police state run by state police as they hunted the accused murderer of one of their own. Roadblocks sprouted like mushrooms after the rain, manned by heavily armed officers who checked every vehicle and questioned every driver. Residents found themselves prisoners in their own homes, advised to stay indoors while the manhunt continued. Schools closed, their playgrounds empty, their hallways echoing with an unusual silence. Businesses shuttered their doors, and tourism—crucial to the Poconos' economy during peak fall foliage season—evaporated as visitors chose safer destinations.

Eric Frein played a deadly game of hide-and-seek with this massive law enforcement apparatus. He was spotted multiple times, ghostly glimpses that sent search teams scrambling toward his last known location, only to find empty forest and the lingering sense that their quarry had been watching them as carefully as they were hunting him. Each sighting generated its own tactical response: resources would converge to secure the area.

The journals Frein kept during this period, later discovered and entered into evidence, reveal a man both surprised by his own endurance and increasingly aware of the inevitable conclusion to his woodland odyssey. In spidery handwriting, he documented his survival techniques, his close calls with search teams and, perhaps most tellingly, his growing astonishment that he had managed to evade capture for so long. There was a curious mixture of pride and resignation in these entries, as if he were simultaneously congratulating himself on his woodcraft while preparing for the martyrdom he seemed to believe awaited him.

The manhunt consumed $10 million in resources and transformed two counties into armed camps where normal life ground to a halt. The psychological toll was as significant as the financial cost: an entire region held its breath while Frein moved through the forest like a malevolent ghost, always one step ahead of his pursuers, always just beyond their reach. Children slept fitfully, their parents keeping loaded guns within easy reach. Hunters stayed home, unwilling to risk being mistaken for the fugitive in the half-light of dawn or dusk. The very woods that had once been a source of recreation and renewal became a place of menace and fear.

The end, when it came, was neither glorious nor particularly dramatic.

The Pocono Mountains had become Eric Frein's fortress, a labyrinth of ridges and valleys, dense undergrowth and rocky outcroppings, abandoned buildings and forgotten trails that offered countless hiding places to a man with the patience and skills to use them. This was a landscape that had sheltered fugitives before—runaway slaves following the Underground Railroad, deserters from various wars, bootleggers during Prohibition. Now it would shelter a cop killer whose survivalist training had prepared him for exactly this kind of extended game of hide-and-seek.

Eric Frein's life as a war reenactor unspooled in somber, shifting shades—a palette tinged with both reverence and unease. In the thickets of rural Pennsylvania, among slopes tangled in vetch and vine, he was less a participant in pageantry than a solitary figure drawn inexorably to the rituals of conflict. His form—thin, quietly intense— was most at home in the dusky woods or beneath the dim shadows of battered canvas tents, where the weight of borrowed uniforms seemed to press him ever nearer to a realm few dared inhabit.

Frein's hands, pale and meticulous, treated every artifact with the care of a priest handling priceless relics. Ex-Yugoslav tunics, boots crusted with memory, packets of Balkan cigarettes; these were the tokens of a private devotion. Others in the reenactment circle shared the hobby, but their enjoyment lacked the fevered gravity that colored Frein's practice. Where most participants sought camaraderie and the thrill of costume, he sought the invisible thread that entwines the living with the dead. He arranged his collections with forensic precision, creating not just a museum but a mausoleum—his own silent sanctuary where the boundaries between imitation and incarnation became impossibly blurred.

The details mattered obsessively. Frein insisted every badge and button mirror its historical counterpart, every cigarette lit with the perfunctory gestures of soldiers long gone. For him, reverence for accuracy was not about scholarship, but about entering a fugue: the act of dressing, the click of buckles, the tightness of a belt became rites unto themselves, each movement a step further from the present and deeper into the echoing corridors of imagined warfare.

Within reenactment circles, Frein inspired both admiration and quiet wariness. His peers noted the air about him: he was not content to reenact a battle for the sake of play but seemed always on the cusp of some deeper transformation. He corrected others with a precision that bordered on impatience, and his eyes, watchful and distant, betrayed the vigilance of someone perpetually attuned to the gravity of violence—its textures, its rules, its silences. If laughter broke out among the group, Frein was more likely to stand aloof, surveying the field as if measuring himself against ghosts.

The psychological implications of his immersion grew hard to ignore. What began as fascination deepened into compulsion, his life outside reenactment becoming hollow by contrast. The rituals of war became an unmoving center, controlling the chaos, reliving the pattern, mastering the unpredictability that in ordinary life left him restless. There was an unspoken but palpable sense that he was not so much learning the past as seeking to rewrite, or perhaps redeem, something fractured within himself. The uniform became armor; the performance, a shield against private disquiet.

To outsiders, his devotion might have seemed romantic, even enviable—a man consumed by his passion. But those who observed closely sensed the shadow lurking behind the ritual. He became increasingly isolated, rebuffing friends who took the hobby lightly and gravitating toward the harsh solemnity of foreign uniforms not out of ideology, but for the way their strangeness matched the estrangement he felt within. The line between preparation and obsession thinned; he was not merely reliving history, but rehearsing for an unnamed conflict he seemed to expect—some storm always gathering just beyond the treeline.

To watch Frein at work was to witness a slow, private unraveling, a steady construction of a world in which he alone was both architect and inhabitant. His reenactments did not end with the bugle or the whistle. They lingered, thread by thread, in the fabric of his days, marking the passage from fantasy to fixation, from commemoration to something grimly anticipatory.

He moved through the landscape, a specter draped in borrowed history, carrying with him the burden of war's relentless echo. In striving to animate the past, he risked becoming its instrument; in fleeing the ordinary, he built a battlefield that existed nowhere but in the shadowed corridors of his own mind.

In the autumn of 2014, the forests of Pennsylvania became the stage for a most peculiar performance—a deadly game of hide-and-seek played between one man and the combined might of American law enforcement. For 48 days, Eric Matthew Frein transformed the dense woodlands of the Pocono Mountains into his private theater, where he would demonstrate an almost artistic mastery of the ancient craft of disappearing.

Those who studied his methods later would marvel at the meticulous preparation that preceded his vanishing act. Long before he pulled the trigger that would make him Pennsylvania's most wanted fugitive, Frein had "planned out his efforts to avoid capture and did research online about how police would be able to track him," law enforcement revealed after a search of his computer. Here was no impulsive flight into the wilderness but rather, the calculated execution of a plan conceived in the quiet moments between his war reenactments, when the line between fantasy and reality had grown gossamer thin.

The investigators who pursued him discovered a man who understood the psychology of the hunt and its mechanics. According to police testimony, he "successfully evaded" their tracking dogs through the simple expedient of "water crossings and terrain conditions," a technique as old as the first escaped slave who understood that running water tells no tales to a bloodhound's nose. Yet this was merely the foundation of his craft.

What truly distinguished Frein's performance was his understanding that a successful fugitive must become, in essence, an actor playing the role of someone who no longer exists. He "used his survivalist skills to live off the land in the dense forests of the Pocono Mountains," and his "knowledge of the terrain and ability to stay off the grid made him a formidable target," court records revealed. The man who had once dressed as a Serbian soldier for weekend war games now inhabited the role with complete authenticity, sustained not by fantasy but by the very real possibility of death.

Perhaps most tellingly, investigators began to realize they were dealing with someone who viewed his evasion as entertainment. Officers spotted Frein dressed all in black on multiple occasions. Authorities came to believe that "some of this is a game to him," suspecting he was showing himself intentionally "in a ploy to taunt them or play games," police expressed in court. Here was the performer's fatal flaw—the need for an audience, even one bent on his destruction.

The physical evidence of his passage told its own story of careful calculation. Court testimony revealed that police had found "empty packs of Serbian cigarettes and soiled diapers believed to belong to Eric Frein" scattered through the forest like breadcrumbs in a fairy tale written by someone with a profoundly dark imagination. The cigarettes spoke to his commitment to his adopted identity; the diapers revealed a mind that had calculated even the most intimate details of extended evasion. What other fugitive would have possessed the foresight—or the psychological discipline—to eliminate even the most basic human needs that might betray his location?

THE ABANDONED JEEP

It was September 15, a Monday, and for James Novak, a day distinguished by private celebration—his 45th wedding anniversary.

But the shadow of the barracks shooting, fresh and terrible, lay over the valley, rendering the ordinary festivities impossible. Propelled by a civic restlessness, a vague but persistent urge to "go out and look for something that might help the state police," Novak turned away from the comfort of his home. He checked his sheds, found them empty, and then, leashing his dog, stepped out of the domestic sphere and into the wilder fringe of his property.

He followed a grassy path that bled away from the manicured safety of the house, moving toward a depression in the land—a large, swampy retaining pond that sat stagnant and silent off Route 402.

There, disrupting the natural emptiness, sat a vehicle.

A green Jeep Cherokee Sport was bogged down in the mire, the murky water up to its hubcaps like a rising tide of bad luck. It was an intrusion, abandoned and silent, sitting about a hundred yards from where Novak stood. He was a local man and he knew the landscape; this object did not belong.

Novak approached. The driver's window gaped open to the elements, a careless vulnerability that suggested panic. Inside, the passenger seat was a landscape of haste—scattered papers, loose change—the detritus of a man who had fled without looking back.

Curiosity, that dangerous impulse, took hold. Protecting his hand with the fabric of his T-shirt—a gesture of forensic instinct—he pried open the rear driver's side door.

The interior yielded its dark secret immediately: an open gun case and the grim clutter of military paraphernalia. The Jeep was no longer a piece of litter; it was a nest. Alarmed by the proximity of the violence, Novak turned back, retracing his steps up the path to the telephone, to the Pennsylvania State Police, and to the end of his quiet morning.

When the troopers arrived, led by Corporal Jeremy Carroll, the swamp gave up its prisoner.

The vehicle was winched from the mud, its contents laid out a biography of the man who had vanished into the trees. The registration spoke the names E. Michael and Deborah

L. Frein. The wallet, heavy with identity, contained the cards of Eric Matthew Frein—driver's licenses, a college ID, a Social Security card. But it was the other items that sketched the portrait of the fanatic: a tube of camouflage face paint, an empty pack of Drina brand cigarettes, and a mini mag flashlight.

Under the rear seat, hiding next to the jack, lay the physical connection to the crime: two empty rifle casings stamped with the mark "AFF 88," the twin brothers of the brass found on the bloodied pavement of the barracks.

But the woods held one more artifact, concealed in the underbrush near the water.

An AK-47 assault rifle was discovered nearby, not discarded carelessly on the ground, but suspended by a string. It was a bizarre, chilling tableau—a precaution against booby traps, or perhaps a final, malicious piece of stagecraft left by a man who believed the war had only just begun.

THE MAKING OF A DOMESTIC TERRORIST

In the deep, shadowed creases of the Pocono Mountains, where the maples bleed jewel tones in the autumn and the silence is thick enough to hold a secret, Eric Matthew Frein found a stage vast enough for his peculiar theater. He was a man of quiet, unremarkable dimensions, slight of build, soft of voice, but in the privacy of the woods, amid the scent of damp earth and decaying leaves, he underwent a transmutation. He ceased to be the aimless college dropout or the dutiful, bullied son. He became "Vuchko," the persona he adopted during his military reenactment and airsoft activities.

To the casual observer, the activities of the Red Alliance—
the group of military simulation enthusiasts Frein
frequented—might have appeared as innocent pageantry,
grown men playing at war with the harmless pop of plastic
pellets. But for Frein, the game was merely a doorway, a
threshold he crossed with a piety that unsettled those who
paid close attention. In 2008, he had founded a unit called
Istočni Vuk, or "Eastern Wolf," a name that rolled off the
tongue with a foreign, dangerous allure. He did not dress in
the crisp, victorious fatigues of the American G.I.; instead,
he draped himself in the drab, mismatched wool of the
Army of Republika Srpska, the uniform of the Bosnian
Serb. His peers in the reenactment circles, men who sought
camaraderie and the thrill of noise, believed this preference
was purely aesthetic—a fondness for the "ragtag look" that
distinguished him from the uniformity of the others.

They were mistaken. They saw a costume; Frein saw a skin.

The evolution of such a man does not begin with the act
of violence, but in the slow, sedimentary accumulation of
grievance. Frein was a child of the suburbs, a "reenactor"
by trade and temperament. There was in him a distinct
yearning for a grandiosity that life had seen fit to deny him.
He lived within the cramped quarters of his parents' home,
yet his mind wandered through the battlefields of Eastern
Europe, draped in the heavy wool of a Serbian paramilitary
uniform. The psychological soil from which such a man
grows is often tilled with perceived grievance and a hunger
for significance.

At the root of his disquiet lay a legacy: the shadow of his
father, a retired U.S. Army major whose stories bore the
legend of heroism and whose standards, it seemed, receded
further the nearer Frein drew to them. The old man's tales
did not inspire emulation so much as they did a kind of
urgent, weary envy; the boy who could not measure up

became the man who stockpiled resentment, its weight multiplying with every retelling. His father, a man who spun false tales of combat heroism, had taught him that the police were growing too powerful—a twisted, familial breeding ground for resentment. The ideology became a convenient, ready-made uniform for his profound sense of personal inadequacy.

This was no sudden fever. The obsession had roots that twisted back years, revealing a mind that had long sought to steal the valor it could not earn. In 2004, a younger Eric Frein had been arrested in New York, charged with thieving uniforms from a World War II reenactment, vanishing into the wind before he could be made to answer for it. It was an early fissure in the mask, a hint that for him, the boundary between the artifact and the act was dangerously permeable.

As the years wore on, the distinction between the man and the mirror image began to dissolve. The "Vuchko" persona was no longer a weekend coat to be shed on Sunday evenings; it was becoming the dominant resident of his soul. A filmmaker who had once observed him noted a certain vibration in the air around such men, a sense that they stood perpetually on the "edge of violence."

Frein lived on that edge. He began to rehearse not just battles, but murder, his fantasies curating a reality where he was not a failure, but a predator stalking prey. The experts found him to be a methodical intelligence who was neither a raging madman nor a simple psychopath, but a "mission-oriented killer" who approached violence with a chilling, clinical detachment. His core delusion was a narcissistic-grandiose conviction that his "solitary, violent act" would be the "spark to ignite a fire" in a nation gone astray. This delusion was an escape from his own personal failure, which he reframed as persecution by a corrupt government, thus transforming his "personal inadequacy" into an "ideological framework" for violence.

He did not see the Pennsylvania State Police as men with families and fatigue; he saw them as symbols—the "blue-clad oppressors" necessary for the completion of his personal myth. By dehumanizing Corporal Bryon Dickson II and Trooper Alex Douglass, Frein allowed himself the moral disengagement necessary to fire from the darkness. He maintained a frightening "clinical separation" from the moral enormity of his acts, even stating his victim knew the risks when he put on the uniform.

THE REENACTOR'S WAR

In the dense woodlands of Pennsylvania, where autumn leaves whispered secrets to those who knew how to listen, Eric Matthew Frein had long practiced the art of becoming someone else entirely. This was not the sort of theatrical transformation one might witness on a Broadway stage, mind you, but something far more meticulous, more consuming.

It was the methodical assumption of a Serbian soldier's identity, complete with the weight of imagined battles and the bitter taste of manufactured grievances.

The man who would one day become the subject of a massive manhunt had, for years prior, been content to wage his wars in miniature. He was part of the Red Alliance, practicing MilSim—military simulation, recreating battles with real uniforms and weapons for recreational purposes. He was particularly interested in Eastern European armies.

There was something almost touchingly earnest about his dedication to authenticity. Fellow reenactors viewed Frein as a serious participant with deep historical knowledge, meticulous in many details such as uniforms, though pragmatic enough to choose a cheaper Chinese-made replica airsoft rifle over one made in Yugoslavia. In the airsoft competitions—similar to paintball except the weapons fired multi-colored plastic BBs—he went by the name "Vuchko."

Yet one wonders now, in retrospect, whether those who knew him recognized the peculiar intensity with which he inhabited these roles. Though he reenacted various roles, Frein preferred to portray Bosnian Serb soldiers. Fellow reenactors believed this preference was not ideological but aesthetic—the way the ragtag look of an ex-Yugoslav field jacket stood out from others.

How little they understood that for some men, the costume eventually becomes the skin.

Frein looked down on casual participants playing "cowboys and Indians," maintaining a sense of humor while remaining serious about historical accuracy. There was, acquaintances would later recall, something almost scholarly about his approach to warfare—even imaginary warfare. He studied. He prepared. He committed himself to the illusion with the fervor of a method actor who has forgotten where the performance ends and reality begins.

To understand the trajectory of the bullet that struck Corporal Dickson, one must first navigate the topography of a different sort of wilderness—not the physical forests of Pike County, but the chimeric landscape of Eric Frein's mind. It was a place where the unremarkable suburban drift of 21st-century America was rejected in favor of a darker, more potent geography.

At the root of his disquiet lay a legacy: the shadow of his father, whose stories bore the legend of heroism and whose standards, it seemed, receded further the nearer Frein drew to them.

In the theater of military simulation, most participants choose to play the hero. They don the crisp, digital camouflage of the American Marine or the stoic olive of the WWII G.I.—costumes of victory. Frein, however, possessed a taste for the losing side.

Why Serbia? Why drape oneself in the mottled wool of a force synonymous with the grim butchery of the Balkans?

For Frein, the allure lay not in the politics of ethnic cleansing, but in the identity of the victim-aggressor. The Bosnian Serb soldier was, in Frein's curating eye, the ultimate pariah—defiant against the world, bombed by NATO, and misunderstood by history, a wolf cornered by the hounds of the West.

It was a seductive narrative for a man who felt himself small and disregarded. By adopting the insignia of the *Istočni Vuk*, Frein was not merely playing a game; he was borrowing a posture of defiance. He was aligning himself with the "noble outcast," transforming his personal failures into a geopolitical struggle.

There is a term in the psychology of role-playing known as "bleed." It describes the perilous membrane where the emotions of the character begin to seep into the player, staining the real world with the passions of the imaginary. For most of the Red Alliance, the game ended when the safety goggles came off. For Frein, the bleed became a hemorrhage.

"Vuchko" was not merely a role; he was a vessel. He was the stronger brother, the bolder spirit. Where Eric was a college dropout living in a bedroom of suspended adolescence, Vuchko was a soldier of fortune, a smoker of Drina cigarettes, a man who spoke the harsh, consonantal tongue of the Serbs.

For Frein, the total immersion that the hobbyist prizes became a total erasure. The boundary lines dissolved. The woods of Pennsylvania ceased to be a state park and transmuted into the Drina Valley.

What distinguished him from other enthusiasts was the way his fantasy life had begun to colonize his reality. He began to rehearse not just battles, but murder, his fantasies curating a reality where he was not a failure, but a predator stalking prey.

The behavioral analysts who would later dissect Frein's psychology saw in his reenactment activities something far more sinister than weekend warrior fantasies. They identified him as a "mission-oriented killer" who approached violence with a chilling, clinical detachment.

The profilers working behind the scenes during his manhunt analyzed how his reenactment background informed his survival tactics in the Pennsylvania woods. They found evidence of his presence through empty packs of Serbian cigarettes and soiled diapers, items that revealed how completely he had maintained his adopted persona even while fleeing justice.

The cigarettes, in particular, spoke to the depth of his commitment to his Serbian soldier identity—a dedication that had transcended hobby and become pathology.

A letter to his parents revealed that "he hoped to spark a revolution by his actions," demonstrating how his reenactment of historical conflicts had merged with grandiose delusions of political significance. The behavioral analysts recognized this pattern: the gradual transformation of a man who had spent years playing at war into someone who believed himself capable of starting one.

One imagines Frein in those final months before his terrible metamorphosis was complete, surrounded by the detritus of his obsession: Serbian cigarettes, military surplus catalogs, photographs of himself in uniform staring back with the cold certainty of someone who had found, at last, his true calling.

The line between performance and reality had not merely blurred. It had been deliberately erased, with the methodical precision of a man who understood that some roles, once assumed, can never be abandoned.

In the end, the woods that had sheltered his fantasies would become the stage for his final, most terrible performance— no longer content with the bloodless pageantry of airsoft pellets and staged retreats, but demanding an audience for a war that existed only in his mind, yet would claim very real victims.

ADVANCED MANHUNT TACTICS

The search for Eric Frein represented one of the most technologically sophisticated manhunts in American law enforcement history. Beyond the conventional methods of grid searches and tracking dogs, authorities deployed cutting-edge equipment that transformed the Pennsylvania wilderness into a high-tech battlefield between man and machine.

The Pennsylvania State Police coordinated what amounted to a small military campaign, utilizing resources that few civilian law enforcement agencies had ever assembled in a single operation. At the height of the search, nearly 1,000 officers from multiple agencies worked in carefully choreographed shifts, their movements coordinated by command centers that resembled military war rooms more than traditional police operations.

Thermal imaging technology proved central to the search strategy. High-resolution FLIR (Forward-Looking Infrared) cameras mounted on helicopters could detect heat signatures as small as a few degrees difference from ambient temperature, capable of spotting a human form even when concealed beneath dense forest canopy. These sophisticated sensors could differentiate between the heat signature of a living person and the residual warmth of recently abandoned campsites, allowing search teams to focus their efforts on areas where Frein had been present within hours rather than days.

Ground-penetrating radar was employed to search cave systems and underground structures where Frein might have taken shelter. This technology, typically used in geological surveys and archeological investigations, could detect void spaces beneath the earth's surface that might provide hiding places invisible to conventional search methods.

Acoustic detection systems were positioned throughout the search area—sensitive microphones capable of detecting and triangulating human sounds from distances of up to two miles. These devices could differentiate between natural forest sounds and human-generated noise, providing early warning when search teams were approaching areas where Frein might be hiding.

The coordination of air and ground assets required unprecedented levels of communication and control. A dedicated command frequency was established for helicopter operations, with flight paths carefully coordinated to prevent interference with ground search patterns. Pilots were equipped with night vision goggles and thermal imaging displays, allowing them to continue operations in complete darkness while maintaining visual contact with ground teams through GPS tracking systems.

Counter-surveillance measures were implemented to prevent Frein from monitoring law enforcement communications. Radio frequencies were changed regularly, and sensitive operational details were communicated through encrypted channels. The assumption that Frein possessed scanning equipment capable of monitoring standard police communications led to the development of communication protocols more typically associated with military operations than civilian law enforcement.

Booby trap detection became a constant concern as the search progressed. Intelligence gathered from Frein's internet searches revealed extensive research into explosive devices and anti-personnel weapons. Every abandoned structure, cache site, and potential hiding place was approached with the assumption that it might be booby trapped. Bomb disposal specialists accompanied search teams whenever they entered buildings or explored areas where Frein had been known to operate.

The integration of military assets marked an unusual aspect of the manhunt. National Guard helicopters provided airlift capabilities for rapid deployment of tactical teams, while their advanced navigation and communication systems allowed for precision operations in difficult terrain. Military surplus equipment, including night vision devices and tactical vehicles, supplemented standard police resources.

CONFLICT

In the crowded, coffee-scented war rooms established in the Blooming Grove firehouse, a friction began to generate its own heat, distinct from the urgency of the hunt. It was the chafing of institution against institution, the grinding of the local against the federal.

To the Pennsylvania State Police, the men in the gray uniforms with the wide-brimmed hats, this was not merely a case; it was a blood debt. One of their own, Corporal Dickson, lay in the earth, and another, Trooper Douglass, remained broken in a hospital bed. The woods that Frein haunted were their jurisdiction, their back yard, their burden. They possessed a primal, possessive need to be the ones to close the handcuffs, to look into the eyes of the man who had shattered their fraternity and say, "We got you."

But as the days bled into weeks and the leaves turned from green to gold to brown, the cavalry arrived, and with it, a complicated salvation. The Federal Bureau of Investigation and the U.S. Marshals came with their endless resources, their "blimps in a box," their cool, detached professionalism. They brought assets the state could not match, but they also brought a different rhythm, a federal cadence that clashed with the local pulse.

A quiet resentment began to simmer in the patrol cars and the chow lines. The "Feds" were viewed by some troopers not as partners, but as interlopers, technicians arriving to fix a machine they did not understand. There was a sense, unspoken but palpable, that the arrival of Washington signaled a failure of Harrisburg. To the trooper who had spent 20 years patrolling these ridges, the federal agent with his GPS and his tactical gear was a tourist in a land of ghosts.

THE GREEN HELL

To the public, the manhunt was a high-tech thriller involving balloons and thermal imagery. To the men on the line, it was a green hell of boredom and misery.

The "line search" is a primitive tactic, a brute-force application of manpower against nature. Troopers stood shoulder to shoulder, a long, gray snake winding through the undergrowth, stepping forward on command. They walked through rhododendron thickets so dense they tore the uniforms and clawed the skin. They walked through poison ivy that left them blistered and itching in the humid heat. They walked through rain that was cold and relentless, soaking through the layers of Kevlar and wool until the shivering was uncontrollable.

Twelve-hour shifts. No talking. Just the sound of boots breaking twigs and the heavy, synchronized breathing of a thousand men.

The exhaustion was physical, but the terror was psychological. It was the fear of "Blue on Blue." In the deep woods, where the light plays tricks and every shadow looks like a man with a rifle, the discipline of fire is the only thing separating a tragedy from a farce. A nervous trooper, a sudden movement, a sneeze—anything could trigger a cascade of gunfire. They walked with their fingers indexed along the trigger guards, trusting the man to their left and the man to their right not to panic.

They were hunting a man who lived in trash, so they became archeologists of garbage. They sifted through the detritus of the forest—the soiled diapers left by a fugitive who had lost all dignity, the empty tuna cans that smelled of metallic decay, the Serbian cigarette packs that were his calling cards. The smell of the manhunt was the smell of wet wool, unwashed bodies, and the faint, sweet rot of the autumn leaves.

And then there were the bears.

The thermal cameras in the helicopters were miracles of technology, picking up the infrared signature of body heat from miles away. But a heat signature has no shape. A "hit" would come over the radio—a glowing white blob in a ravine. The adrenaline would spike. The tactical teams would converge, hearts hammering against their ribs, weapons raised, ready to end it. They would creep through the brush, surrounding the target, only to have a black bear, confused and grumpy, lumber out of the darkness. The adrenaline crash that followed was a physical blow, leaving them more exhausted than before.

To the public, watching from the safety of their living rooms, the manhunt was a high-tech thriller of thermal cameras and hovering balloons. But to the men on the line, the troopers conscripted into the green hell, it was a misery of medieval proportions. They moved through the rhododendron slicks like a single, gray-clad organism, a thousand feet crushing the damp earth in a synchronized trudge that led nowhere. And the woods did not welcome them.

BUCK HILL FALLS

On the morning of September 26, 2014, the mist that clung to the Pocono ridges had not yet lifted when the Pennsylvania State Police, moving with the heavy, synchronized tread of men expecting war, breached the perimeter of the Buck Hill Falls Inn.

It was a Friday, the 14th day of the manhunt, and the target was Eric Frein, a survivalist specter who had turned the dense Pennsylvania woods into a theater of evasion. But the stage for this particular act was not a forest but a tomb—a 400-room colossus of gray stone that had sat rotting in the damp mountain air for nearly a quarter of a century.

A melancholy giant erected in 1901, the inn had begun its life as a modest wooden hostelry, a "simple retreat" for Philadelphia Quakers who sought to escape the city's soot for the moral clarity of fresh air and cold water. But simplicity is a difficult virtue to maintain in the face of success. Over the decades, the structure had calcified into a fortress of masonry, expanding in 1926 to accommodate the worldly appetites of the very rich. It was a place of aggressive leisure, where harpsichords tinkled in the white linen dining room and where the sun, filtered through the famous retractable glass roof of the indoor swimming pool, once dappled the chlorine-blue water in which captains of industry floated, buoyant and safe.

Now, the water was gone, replaced by a sediment of dead leaves and shattered glass. The tactical teams, 12 units strong, moved through the "New West Wing" and the fire-scarred library, their rifle-mounted flashlights cutting beams through the gloom. They found a world stripped of its vanity. The wallpaper, peeling in long, sunburned shreds, hung like dead skin from the lath; the floorboards, warped by years of leaking slate roofs, groaned under the weight of Kevlar and ceramic plating. The silence of the place was absolute, save for the sharp crack of doors being kicked in—Room 302, Room 303, Room 304—a rhythmic violence that echoed down the serpentine corridors.

The locals, and a sensational production by MTV, had long ago populated these halls with ghosts. They whispered of 73 murders, of a maid who had hanged herself in a fit of despair, of ley lines that drew darkness to the property like iron filings to a magnet. But the troopers were not hunting ectoplasm. They were hunting a man who had, in better times, treated this decay as a playground. Frein, a student of abandonment, had allegedly prowled these very corridors in the years before his crime, studying the architecture of ruin, perhaps imagining himself the king of this hollow castle.

The searchers moved deeper, past the cavernous stone fireplaces where logs the size of men once burned, and out onto the enormous covered porch, where the view of the mountains remained breathtakingly indifferent to the human drama unfolding below. They checked the tunnels, the basements, the nooks where a man might fold himself into the shadows. They found nothing. No sniper, no survivalist, no trace of the fugitive. The Buck Hill Falls Inn, for all its rumored horrors, offered up no secrets that day. It simply swallowed the noise of the search and, when the helicopters finally turned back toward the barracks, settled once more into the heavy, wet silence of its slow and relentless creep of decay.

THE PROTECTORS

Kevin Thomas was a man of two worlds, straddling the line between the sterile, fluorescent order of the University of Pennsylvania's trauma, helicopter bays, and the chaotic, mud-slicked theater of federal law enforcement. Technically, he was a civilian—a manager of the PennSTAR Critical Care Team—but to the agents of the Philadelphia FBI, he was simply "Doc." For 25 years, a unique marriage had existed between the Bureau and the university, a program born of the realization that when special agents kick down doors, they require something more than a first-aid kit. They require surgeons. They require paramedics. They require men like Kevin Thomas—vetted, credentialed, and embedded into the stack, ready to fix the broken things that violence leaves behind.

Kevin Thomas is a paramedic.

It was a strange, grim destiny that brought him to the Poconos in that warm September of 2014. The terrain was not foreign to him; it was a landscape of memory. His family held a cabin in Blooming Grove, a mere two miles from where the state troopers had fallen. He knew the winding roads, the treacherous deception of the woods. Years prior, during a blinding snowstorm on an unplowed road, he had forged a friendship with a local Blooming Grove cop—a chance meeting in a whiteout that ended with shared coffee and a radio patch. Now, that same radio frequency crackled with the frantic, static-laced electricity of a manhunt.

When the call came, the page from the Philadelphia FBI was terse. They were putting a ground deployment together. Two troopers were down. The woods were full of shadows. Thomas packed his gear—the bulletproof vest, the medical rucksack, the boots—and drove north; not to a hospital, but to war.

His war began in the sky.

Because the ground teams were PennSTAR qualified, they needed a medic who brought his own helmet, a man who spoke the language of aviation. Thomas was detailed to Omaha 7, a Customs and Border Patrol helicopter crew that had flown north from the humid heat of Miami. They were piloting UH-60 Black Hawks, birds of prey designed for the desert, now hunting in the dense, dying foliage of Pennsylvania.

They flew out of Avoca, near Scranton, staging at an airport that felt less like a transit hub and more like a forward operating base. The mission was a monotonous, high-stakes loop of chasing ghosts. They hunted radio signals; they hunted movement. At night, they tried to use FLIR to pierce the canopy. But the Poconos were alive, teeming with heat signatures that mocked their technology. A deer, a bear, a U.S. Marshal creeping through the undergrowth—on the thermal screen, they were all just glowing specters in the dark.

The woods were playing tricks on everyone. On the ground, the tension was a taut wire, humming with the expectation of gunfire. Transitioning from the air to the ground, Kevin Thomas found himself riding in an FBI Suburban, a roving ambulance amid a convoy of armor. They staged at the Coolbaugh Township Elementary School, an abandoned structure that had been repurposed into a fortress. There was food, there were cots, there was 24/7 security, but outside the perimeter, the world was uncertain.

They searched the grand, decaying resorts of a bygone era. Buck Hill Falls Inn, with its 300 rooms, loomed like a gothic monument to the manhunt. Thomas, alongside teams of FBI agents, swept the hotel room by room, hour by hour. It was surreal. The night before, unable to sleep in the adrenaline haze, Thomas had watched a television program, *Paranormal Adventures*, which claimed the hotel was haunted. Now, a flashlight beam cutting the dust, he cleared the same hallways, half expecting a ghost but hunting a killer.

The search was a series of adrenaline spikes followed by crushing nothingness. They would breach a cabin, hearts hammering, anticipating a muzzle flash, only to find the remnants of a life on the run—a can of beans, a depression in a mattress where a body had rested, a fast-food wrapper. The phantom was always one step ahead, perhaps aided, the agents whispered, by sympathizers who left supplies in the dark.

In the thickets of laurel, the paranoia was palpable. Once, near a fire road, the radio screamed, *"Contact! Contact!"* Men ran, weapons raised, tearing through the brush toward the movement. Thomas, positioning himself to treat the wounded, watched as the suspect burst from the greenery. It was a bear. Just a bear, frightened by the invasion of humans.

Yet, amid the frustration, there was a profound, quiet brotherhood. To the agents—men from Saginaw, from Miami, from the hardened streets of Philadelphia—Thomas was their lifeline. Before a hoist operation, where Thomas would dangle 200 feet below the Black Hawk on a thin cable, vulnerable as a worm on a hook, the gunner leaned over. His face was obscured by the machinery of war, but his voice was clear.

"Hi, Doc," the gunner said. "I'm the gunner behind you. And I have your back."

For 20 days, Kevin Thomas lived this life. He slept in fits, ate when he could, and moved with the singular purpose of the hunt. He had searched the Pocono Airport three times. He had walked the very ground where the end would eventually come. But the climax, when it arrived, belonged to someone else.

He was scheduled to return on Halloween morning. He had washed his gear, packed his Jeep, and prepared to ascend the mountain once more. Then, the text came from his boss: **We got him.**

The words were hard to process. After 48 days of tension, of fear, of false tips and sympathetic locals sending them in circles, it was over. Eric Frein was in custody, found in a hangar at the very airport Thomas had cleared days before, huddled under a canopy with fresh food.

Thomas felt a strange hollowness. There was relief, certainly—no more officers would bleed in the leaves—but there was no closure. He had not seen the handcuffs click. He had not seen the man walked out. He had only the silence of the aftermath, the memory of the wind in the open door of a Black Hawk, and the faces of the men who had looked at him and called him "Doc."

The economic devastation was quiet but ruinous. Small business owners, the proprietors of diners and bait shops who relied on the influx of "flatlanders" to pad their ledgers for the coming winter, watched their doorways with desperate hope. But the bells did not ring. The customers, frightened by the looping news reels of a sniper on the loose, stayed away. A diner owner in Canadensis, wiping down a counter that had not seen a crumb in hours, remarked that the killer did not need to shoot anyone else to destroy the town; he simply had to remain hidden. Bankruptcy did not arrive with a bang, but with the slow, suffocating accumulation of empty days.

Inside the homes, the atmosphere was subterranean. Families retreated to basements, sleeping on mattresses dragged down from the airy vulnerability of second-floor bedrooms. The school buses stopped running. Halloween, the high holy day of childhood, was canceled by decree. A generation of children in the Poconos learned that monsters were not creatures of latex and corn syrup, but men who looked like their fathers, hiding in the ferns.

With a thousand officers scouring the underbrush, adrenaline became a dangerous intoxicant. The woods were full of shadows, and every shadow looked like Eric Frein. There were moments—terrifying, breathless moments—when the innocent brushed against the lethal. A hiker, seeking a moment of peace, stumbling upon a tactical team; a resident, stepping out to check a fuse box, finding himself illuminated by the blinding beam of a weapon-mounted light.

Mistaken identities were the currency of the day. A man walking his dog, a teenager in a hooded sweatshirt—anyone who fit the vague, skeletal description of the survivalist became a target until proven otherwise. The air hummed with the potential for tragic error, a fear that the next headline would not be the capture of a fugitive, but the accidental martyrdom of a neighbor.

Consider the Barrett family, living in a cul-de-sac that abutted the very state game lands where the manhunt raged. Their experience, recorded in the mental diary of a mother trying to keep panic at bay, offers a stark counterpoint to the cold, scribbled justifications found in Frein's own water-stained journals.

By the 12th day, inside the Barrett house, the heat was turned up to chase away the chill, but the curtains were drawn tight against the world. The mother noted that the pizza delivery boy refused to come up the driveway, leaving dinner to be a silent affair of leftovers. They watched movies with the volume low, as if laughter might attract the attention of the devil outside.

As the siege dragged into its 30th day, the Barrett children asked if they could play in the yard, but the answer was a perpetual no. The father paced the kitchen, watching the helicopter circle overhead, its rotor wash shaking the window panes, feeling like a prisoner in the home he had worked 20 years to own.

Meanwhile, in the damp earth beneath a fallen tree, Frein shivered in a hole, opening a tin of tuna. He was the king of his own small, freezing kingdom, writing of revolution while his socks rotted on his feet. He smoked a Drina cigarette, the smoke curling up to join the mist, believing himself a soldier on a grand campaign.

He was hunting too—not for game, but for Wi-Fi signals, a technological parasite feeding on the very society he claimed to reject. He was dirty, diminished, a "revolutionary" scrounging for batteries in the dark.

When the news finally broke on day 48, the lights in the Barrett house blazed on, every single one of them, a defiant beacon against the dark. The siege was broken. The phantom was revealed to be just a man, handcuffed and small, dragged from an abandoned hangar. But as the mother looked out at the treeline, she knew the woods would never look the same. The innocence of the landscape had been spent, paid out to a man who bought his infamy with their fear.

The devastation at Blooming Grove, a violence both remote and impossibly close, had its corollary in the sudden, unnerving paralysis of ordinary life. At East Stroudsburg South, an elementary school anchored in an urban district many miles distant from the precise geography of the calamity, the terror had nevertheless taken root. There, in Mrs. Kaitlyn Lopez's fourth-grade class, Little Natalie Skusa sat in silent, persistent dread. Though the tragedy was far from her doorstep, the school had sealed itself against the unknown: the classroom doors were locked fast, and the customary noise and freedom of recess were exchanged for the hollow, contained quiet of an indoor confinement.

"I was anxious, confused," Natalie reflected recently upon that peculiar season of fear. "I needed my sister to go with me to take out the garbage." The common, unremarkable acts of a child's life had suddenly required an accomplice.

THE SEASON OF FEAR

In the autumn of 2014, the rolling hills and dense woodlands of Pennsylvania's Pike County and southerly neighboring Monroe County became, quite suddenly, a prison without bars—a vast outdoor cell where 30,000 souls found themselves unwilling inmates in someone else's deadly game. For 48 days, the specter of Eric Frein transformed an entire region into a landscape of perpetual anxiety, where the simple act of stepping outside one's door became a calculated risk, and the changing colors of October leaves seemed less like nature's artistry than camouflage for unseen eyes.

The transformation was as swift as it was complete. Schools were closed, residents were advised to stay indoors, and the region experienced a state of tension and anxiety. What had been, mere days before, communities preparing for the gentle rituals of fall—Friday night football games, harvest festivals, the quiet pleasure of raking leaves—became something altogether more sinister. The entire region was disrupted, suffering blocked roads, school closings, game cancellations, and lost fall-season tourism dollars. People lived in fear that Frein would train his sights on someone in the search zone.

The children, perhaps, suffered most acutely from this sudden rupture in the ordinary fabric of their lives. Students in the Pocono Mountain School District returned to school under tight security Tuesday morning as police continued to search for Eric Frein, their young minds struggling to comprehend why armed officers now stood guard at the places where they had once felt safest. The school district was forced to lay out "a variety of measures" that transformed classrooms from sanctuaries of learning into fortified positions against an enemy who might materialize from any shadow.

For the adults, the psychological toll manifested in different ways. Fear. Anxiety. Surprise. Residents described what it was like living inside the search area for suspected cop killer Eric Matthew Frein. These simple words—scared, anxious, surprised—seem almost inadequate to capture the peculiar terror of knowing that somewhere in the familiar woods where one had walked dogs and picked berries, a predator waited with the patience of a hunter and the skills of a soldier.

The very infrastructure of daily life buckled under the weight of collective fear. Heavily armed Pennsylvania State Police troopers "guarded an entrance into a neighborhood" and were "checking every vehicle leaving," without any warrants or probable cause. Citizens found themselves subjected to searches and scrutiny in their own neighborhoods, the Constitution temporarily suspended in service of the greater good of community survival.

As the silence deepened in the woods, the noise grew in the town. The media vans arrived first, white behemoths with satellite dishes turned upward like prayer wheels, parking on the manicured lawns of Barrett Township with the entitlement of an invading army. They brought with them the bright, hot glare of the 24-hour news cycle, illuminating the quiet corners of the Poconos until the shadows seemed to stretch and distort. In the vacuum of official silence—for the Pennsylvania State Police spoke only in the clipped, sterile dialect of the press release—rumor rushed in to fill the void.

It was a season of whispers. At the diner counters and in the aisles of the grocery store, the truth was dissected and reassembled into grotesque new shapes. He was in the school. He was in the church steeple. He was watching from the tree line. The "Facebook detectives," safe behind their glowing screens, spun elaborate webs of conspiracy, transforming a college dropout into a mythical super soldier, a "Rambo" of the ridges capable of vanishing into the bark of an oak tree. The locals, men and women who had known the woods all their lives, found themselves strangers in their own geography, looking at the familiar maples and seeing not the autumn turn, but the hiding place of a monster.

As the days stretched into weeks, local residents grew frustrated with the search. The initial shock had given way to a grinding, persistent anxiety—the kind that settles into one's bones and changes the very rhythm of breathing. Mothers developed the habit of counting their children multiple times each day. Men found themselves checking and rechecking door locks with the obsessive precision of ritual. The elderly, particularly, seemed to age years in the span of weeks, their faces taking on the hollow-eyed look of people who had seen too much of what the world could do.

In the high, hard country of the Poconos, where the maples ignite in a sudden, violent crimson before surrendering to the November grays, the autumn of 2014 was a season suspended in amber—not the amber of preservation, but of entrapment. For 48 days, the residents of Pike and Monroe Counties lived within the borders of a geography that had ceased to be Pennsylvania and had become, simply, "The Zone."

It was a time when the Constitution, that sturdy parchment of rights, seemed to curl and wither in the damp autumn air, replaced by the immediate, muscular reality of martial law in all but name.

The roads, once the arteries of commerce and quiet commute, were now choked with the blue and gray of state authority. To drive down Route 402 was to submit oneself to a gauntlet of suspicion. Officers, their eyes rimmed with the red fatigue of sleepless shifts, peered into the sanctity of family sedans and plumber's vans with the same accusatory glare. They checked vehicles "without any warrants or probable cause," a phrase that belongs to the sterile lexicon of the courtroom but, on the asphalt, felt like an invasion.

The "Frein Zone" was a peculiar legal twilight where the Fourth Amendment was treated as a luxury the community could no longer afford, a casualty of the bullet that had struck Corporal Dickson. There was resentment, certainly—a low, grumbling boil among the locals who felt the hot breath of the State on their necks. Town halls became theaters of anxiety, where the rights of the citizen clashed with the survival instinct of the herd. Men who had spent their lives distrusting the government found themselves opening their trunks to it, offering up their privacy as a tithe for protection against the phantom in the woods. They hated the intrusion, yet they locked their doors and prayed the troopers would not leave.

The domestic texture of the siege was woven from a silence that felt unnatural in a season usually loud with the crack of rifles. It was hunting season, or it should have been. But the woods, the lifeblood of the local culture and economy, were closed. The hunters, men who had waited all year for the frost to harden the ground, sat in their living rooms, their rifles oiled and racked, staring at television screens that showed their own back yards occupied by armored personnel carriers.

THE GATED COMMUNITY

It was a gradual, creeping frost that descended upon Barrett Township, a chill unrelated to the turning of the calendar or the shortening of days. In the hamlets of Canadensis and Price Township, the autumn of 2014 brought with it a peculiar and heavy silence, the sort of quiet that falls not when nature sleeps, but when a community holds its collective breath. The paved roads, usually ribbons of commerce and neighborly transit, had been transformed into the arteries of an occupation. The landscape, once defined by the sprawling liberty of the Poconos—where a man might walk from his back porch into the endless green without meeting a soul—had been redrawn by the hard, unyielding geometry of the police perimeter.

For 48 days, the citizens of Pike and Monroe Counties lived within a parenthesis of history, a suspended reality where the Constitution of the United States seemed to have been placed, gently but firmly, on a high shelf, out of reach. The "Frein Zone," as the television reporters called it with their breathless, practiced gravity, was a place where the ordinary rules of civil existence had been superseded by the singular, driving imperative of the hunt.

At the intersection of Route 447 and the winding backroads, the friction between the protectors and the protected began to chafe. Here, the checkpoint was not merely a traffic stop but a ritual of submission. Returning from the grocery store with milk and bread, a resident would find the road barred by men in body armor, their faces obscured by the grim indifference of duty, their hands resting near the triggers of automatic rifles. The trunk must be popped, the interior illuminated, the driver's license surrendered. There were no warrants presented, no murmurs of probable cause. There was only the flashlight's beam cutting through the privacy of the vehicle and the silent, heavy implication that in a time of war, liberty is a luxury the besieged cannot afford.

"It gets to you," said Martin Kessler, a retired machinist who lived within the perimeter. "The first week, you wave. You say, 'Get him, boys.' You bring them coffee. The third week, you stop waving. The fifth week, you resent the flashlight in your eyes. You start to feel less like a citizen and more like a suspect in your own driveway."

This resentment was a slow-acting poison. In the town halls and the diners—those that remained open—the talk shifted from the horror of the crime to the heaviness of the response. There were whispers of the "Constitutional Gray Zone," a phrase that moved from the lips of lawyers to the mouths of hunters and housewives. Was it legal? Was it right? To search a man's shed without asking? To bar a woman from her own street because a sensor had tripped in the woods? Fueled by adrenaline and the desperate need to avenge their fallen brother, the police saw the community as a battlespace; fueled by anxiety and a growing claustrophobia, the community began to see the police not as saviors but as jailers.

Inside the homes, the siege mentality took on a domestic texture, a reordering of the intimate habits of life. Consider the house of the Weaver family, a modest ranch set back against the treeline in Price Township. Before September, the doors were rarely locked until midnight; the windows were left open to catch the mountain breeze. Now, the house was a fortress.

Thomas Weaver, a man who had hunted these woods since he was a boy of 12, sat in his living room with a loaded shotgun across his knees—a tableau repeated in a hundred living rooms across the county. He had lost his season. The woods, his cathedral, were closed. The deer moved through the undergrowth with impunity, while the hunters sat indoors, prisoners of a different sort of prey.

"You don't sleep," Weaver said, his voice dropping to a murmur so as not to wake his children, who had been moved from their bedrooms to the interior hallway, sleeping in sleeping bags on the floor, away from the windows. "You listen. You listen for a footstep on the porch, a branch snapping. And then you hear a helicopter, low and loud, shaking the plates in the cupboard, and you know they're out there. But who is 'they'? Is it the killer? Or is it the thousand men looking for him? In the dark, it doesn't matter. It's just noise and fear."

The terror of the occupation was not merely existential; it was economic, a slow bleeding of the region's lifeblood. The Poconos, dependent on the leaf-peepers and the weekenders, saw its economy wither on the vine. The "Frein Zone" was a brand, a scarlet letter that warned away the tourists.

At the Mountainhome Diner, the booths sat empty, the coffee pots stewing on the burners. "I lost forty percent of my business in October," said the owner, a woman named Helen, wiping a counter that was already clean. "People are afraid to come up. And the locals? They're afraid to come out. I have waitresses who can't pay their rent because there are no tips. Who do I sue for that? The killer? The state police? It's a disaster that nobody will pay for."

The tension birthed a dangerous confusion, a blurring of lines. With a thousand officers on edge, seeing the ghost of Eric Frein in every shadow, the potential for tragedy multiplied. There were stories, passed in hushed tones, of mistaken identities—of the innocent hiker held at gunpoint, of the teenager walking home in a hoodie who found himself illuminated by the spotlight of a hovering helicopter, ordered to his knees in the dirt.

One such incident involved a local contractor, a man of similar height and build to the fugitive, who made the mistake of walking his property line at dusk to check a fence. He recounted, with a trembling hand, the moment the trees seemed to come alive, the shout of "Show me your hands!" echoing from the brush, the terrifying realization that he was a split-second, a twitch of a finger, away from becoming collateral damage in the state's war.

"I stood there," he recalled, "and I thought, 'This is it. I'm going to die in my own back yard because I look like him.' And when they lowered the guns, when they saw I wasn't him, there was no apology. Just anger. Anger that I was there. Anger that I wasn't the one they wanted. We were all just in the way."

This was the texture of the occupation: a community compressed by fear from within and authority from without. The schools, when they finally reopened, were no longer places of learning but garrisons, with armed troopers patrolling the hallways and recess held indoors, the laughter of children swallowed by the safety of brick and mortar. The innocence of the small town, the belief that the bad things happened elsewhere—in the cities, on the news—had been irrevocably shattered.

And so, while Eric Frein scribbled his delusions in a notebook deep in the rhododendrons, imagining himself a revolutionary, the people of Pike and Monroe Counties wrote their own diary of the siege. It was a chronicle not of grand battles, but of small, daily erosions—of rights suspended, of trust frayed, of the profound and exhausting weight of living in a world where every stranger was a threat and every protector was a potential danger. They waited for the capture not with the thirst for vengeance, but with the desperate, weary hope that the army would leave, the roadblocks would lift, and they might, at long last, unlock their doors.

FEAR IN THE WOODLANDS

The transformation of Barrett Township was not sudden, like a thunderclap, but accumulating, like a heavy, wet snow that breaks the boughs of the pines. The silence of the Poconos, that deep, resinous quiet that the mountain people hoard like gold, was shattered not by the singular crack of Eric Frein's rifle, but by the thundering, mechanical response of the State.

To the residents of Canadensis, people accustomed to a privacy so thick you could wrap yourself in it, the arrival of the Pennsylvania State Police was less a rescue and more an invasion. They came in a steel tide—armored BearCats groaning up the narrow, winding roads, helicopters beating the air into a submission that rattled the china in grandmothers' cupboards, and a sea of gray uniforms that washed over the manicured lawns and the wild bramble alike.

The friction was intimate, born of a clash between two distinct species of American life: the rural individualist and the paramilitary bureaucrat. It played out in the glare of the floodlights that turned night into a harsh, antiseptic day, bleaching the mystery out of the woods and ruining the sleep of working men and women.

"Show me your ID!" a trooper would bark, his hand hovering near his holster, his eyes obscured behind mirrored glass, stopping a woman who had lived on that road since before the trooper was born. She was merely trying to fetch a gallon of milk but suddenly, at the end of her own driveway, she was a suspect, a variable in a tactical equation. The locals, men who knew every deer trail and hidden creek, found themselves barred from their own back yards, told by nervous young men from Philadelphia or Pittsburgh that the woods—their woods—were now a "hot zone."

There was a sullen resentment brewing in the diners and the post office queues. It was not that they did not want Frein caught; they feared the assassin in the ferns as much as anyone. But they resented the implication that they were collateral damage in a war they had not asked for. They watched as troopers trampled their azaleas and set up listening posts in their gazebos. They felt the indignity of having their trunks popped and searched by men who looked at the dense, impenetrable foliage with a mixture of arrogance and terrified bewilderment.

The police saw the community as a landscape of potential hiding spots; the community saw the police as an occupying army that did not know a hemlock from a hickory. It was a friction of proximity—the troopers sleeping in the local school, the armed patrols marching past the bus stops—a constant, grinding reminder that the normal order of things had been suspended and that in the eyes of the law, the innocent and the guilty were, for the moment, indistinguishable.

The search for Eric Frein took 48 days. It cost nearly $12 million and altered people's lives. But the true cost—the psychological scar tissue that would remain long after the manhunt ended—proved far more difficult to calculate. For many residents, the autumn of 2014 would forever remain the season when their sense of safety died, when they learned that evil could emerge from the most familiar places, wearing a face they might have passed in the grocery store or sat beside in church.

The manhunt's end brought relief, certainly, but also a kind of spiritual exhaustion—the bone-deep weariness of people who had spent too many weeks sleeping with one ear open, who had aged a year for every day of October, who had discovered that the thin veneer of civilization could be stripped away by a lone man with a rifle and a grievance.

The woods remained beautiful, the mountains still majestic, but innocence, once lost, could never be fully restored.

In the humid, leaf-cluttered depths of the Barrett Township woods, a phantom began to breathe. During those 48 days, the man known as Eric Frein ceased to be a mere mortal—a lean, Mohawk-scalped fugitive—and ascended into the chilly heights of local mythology. To the frightened citizenry of Canadensis, huddled behind double-bolted doors while helicopter searchlights swept their bedroom walls, he had become a specter of supernatural competence: a "Rambo" of the Poconos who could melt into the bark of an oak tree or outrun a bloodhound without snapping a twig.

The legends grew like fungus in the damp. Neighbors whispered over coffee of a figure standing motionless in the moonlight, a silhouette that offered a mocking, slow-motion salute to the police cruisers before dissolving into the mist. They spoke of a woodland ninja who survived on berries and venom, a tactical genius who taunted the state's massive machinery with the casual arrogance of a boy playing hide-and-seek. In the mind of the public, the "Vuchko" persona had fully eclipsed the man; he was no longer a murderer, but a predatory ghost haunting the very porch steps of civilization.

But the earth, unlike the imagination, is a meticulous record-keeper of our humiliations. When the state troopers finally stumbled upon the sanctuaries where the phantom had rested, they did not find the Spartan bivouac of a warrior-king. Instead, they found the pathetic debris of a man unraveling in the cold.

There, amid the ferns, lay the stinking evidence of a desperate, unglamorous reality: piles of soiled adult diapers used by a man too terrified of his own scent or the sound of his movement to leave his hiding spot to relieve himself.

The forest floor was littered with the crumpled yellow packs of Drina cigarettes—harsh, Serbian tobacco that served as a pungent trail of breadcrumbs for the investigators. There were no grand feasts of the land, only the sticky remnants of Ramen noodles and canned tuna consumed in the dark.

The "Rambo" of the Poconos had not been a master of the wild; he was merely a frightened creature burrowing into the muck, leaving behind a trail of trash and human waste. The myth was a towering edifice of granite and shadow, but the truth, as it so often is, was written in the dirt—a small, messy story of a man who had traded his humanity for a rifle, only to find that the woods offered no dignity to a killer, only a place to rot in his own filth.

THE SIEGE OF THE INNOCENTS

The Poconos in autumn are a landscape of violent beauty, a geography where the maples and oaks immolate themselves in rioting shades of crimson and burnt orange. It is a season that usually belongs to the tourists, the "leaf-peepers" who drive up from the gray confinement of Philadelphia and New York to breathe the air and marvel at the dying year. But in 2014, the season did not belong to the tourists. It belonged to the state.

The transformation of Barrett Township and its neighboring hamlets was swift and total. The topography of leisure— the winding country roads, the hunting cabins, the roadside diners—was overlaid by the rigid geometry of a military occupation. The region became known, in the shorthand of the news chyrons, as "The Frein Zone," a designation that sounded less like a neighborhood and more like a quarantine.

For the residents, the transition from citizen to suspect happened at the end of every driveway. The checkpoints became the new landmarks of their lives. State troopers, clad in the heavy armor of urban warfare, stood sentinel at roadblocks that severed the arteries of the community. To go to the grocery store was to negotiate a checkpoint; to return with a gallon of milk was to prove, once again, that you belonged in your own home.

The school buses, usually the yellow vessels of morning exuberance, were now somber transports. They moved through the corridors of trees with armed escorts, the children pressing their faces against the glass to watch the men in camouflage who watched them back. At stops, heavily armed officers would board, their eyes scanning the rows of seats, checking beneath the vinyl benches for the stowaway monster. For the school children, it was a terrifying novelty that slowly calcified into routine; for the parents watching from their porches, it was a daily violation, a reminder that their safety was purchased at the price of their privacy.

Life inside the perimeter acquired a surreal, muted quality. The ordinary sounds of the suburbs—the lawnmowers, the barking dogs, the slamming of car doors—were dampened by a collective anxiety. People moved quickly from house to car, casting nervous glances toward the treeline, where the forest, once a border of privacy, had become a wall of eyes.

THE ECONOMICS OF FEAR

If the psychological toll was heavy, the economic toll was a slow strangulation. The manhunt had coincided with the region's harvest, the few crucial weeks when the local economy gorged itself on tourism to survive the coming winter. But fear is bad for business.

The bed-and-breakfasts, usually booked solid with couples seeking rustic romance, sat empty, their "No Vacancy" signs turned around to plead for guests who would never come. The cancellation calls came in a relentless tide—polite regrets from city people who preferred their autumn foliage without the accompaniment of Black Hawk helicopters.

In the diners and the general stores, the resentment began to curdle. It was a complex anger, directed first at the phantom in the woods, but inevitably spilling over onto the occupiers. The diner owner, staring out at a parking lot filled only with police cruisers, calculated his losses in the thousands. The police were eating, certainly, but they were a grim clientele, and their mere presence chased away the regulars.

"We support the police," a hardware store owner might say, leaning over a counter that had seen no commerce that morning. "But they're killing us. He's killing us, and they're helping him do it."

The frustration was palpable in the town meetings, where weary spokesmen for the police tried to placate a population that was bleeding money. The residents wanted the killer caught, but they also wanted their lives back. They wanted the roadblocks gone. They wanted the helicopters to stop shaking the shingles off their roofs at three in the morning. They wanted to stop showing identification to drive down a road their grandfathers had paved.

THE MONSTERS IN THE SHADOWS

In this pressurized atmosphere, the mind began to play tricks. Paranoia, fed by the 24-hour news cycle and the visible presence of the manhunt, bloomed like a dark fungus.

The police hotlines were flooded with the testimonies of the terrified.

An elderly woman in Canadensis, her eyesight failing but her fear acute, swore she saw a figure moving in her garden shed. The tactical teams descended, weapons drawn, surrounding the small wooden structure with the precision of a raid on a terrorist cell. They found nothing but a startled groundhog and the dust of years.

On the ridges, shadows became silhouettes. A trick of the moonlight on a swaying birch tree became a sniper. A hiker's discarded jacket became a campsite. The police were obligated to chase every phantom, to run down every ghost story born of anxiety. They kicked down doors and swept through basements, finding only the innocent debris of ordinary lives.

The community had entered a state of collective hyper-vigilance. Every rustle in the dry leaves was a footstep; every dog barking in the distance was an alarm. The woods, which had been their playground and their solace, were now the citizens' enemy. They looked at the treeline and saw not nature, but the hiding place of a man who had proven that he could strike without warning and vanish without a trace.

THE SILENCE OF OCTOBER 31

The tension culminated on the last night of October. Halloween in the Poconos is usually a riot of small terrors, a parade of plastic skeletons and sugar-fueled laughter. But in the autumn of 2014, Halloween, the holiday of manufactured fear, arrived in a town paralyzed by the real thing.

The decision had come down from the township supervisors, men with gray faces and heavy responsibilities, a bureaucratic decree that carried the weight of a funeral sentence: Halloween was canceled. There would be no trick-or-treating. The risk was too high. The woods were too close The thought of children wandering the dark streets, masked and vulnerable, while a cop killer with a sniper rifle remained at large, was a nightmare no official was willing to sanction.

And so, October 31 fell upon Barrett Township with a silence that was almost liturgical. The streets, which should have been alive with the shrieks of vampires and the giggles of princesses, lay desolate under the cold moon. Porches remained dark. Pumpkins sat unlit on the stoops like blind, orange sentinels guarding nothing, for to light a jack-o'-lantern was to invite attention—and attention was the one thing nobody wanted.

The silence was absolute. It was not the quiet of peace, but the quiet of holding one's breath. Inside the houses, families sat behind drawn blinds, the bags of candy purchased weeks ago sitting unopened in cupboards. Parents tried to distract their children with movies or games, but the absence of the ritual hung in the room.

Outside, the wind moved through the empty streets, rattling the dry leaves across the pavement. A police cruiser rolled slowly past, its headlights sweeping the yards where the plastic skeletons and fake cobwebs hung limp and disregarded. The irony was bitter and complete: the town had dressed up for a horror story it was pretending to enjoy, only to find itself trapped in a horror story it could not escape.

In the end, Eric Frein, huddling in his damp hole somewhere in the black pine barrens, achieved something more profound than evasion. He had stolen the night. He had taken the innocent pageantry of childhood and replaced it with the cold, adult reality of dread. He was nowhere to be seen and yet, on this silent, wind-blown Halloween, he was everywhere.

THE QUIET MAN NEXT DOOR

In the aftermath of the manhunt, when the Pennsylvania State Police had finally dragged their quarry from the abandoned airport hangar and the helicopters had ceased their endless circling over the Pocono Mountains, the neighbors began to open up. They spoke hesitantly at first, as people do when they discover that evil has been living quietly among them, wearing the unremarkable mask of the ordinary.

Eric Frein's neighbors described him as eccentric, though one suspects that "eccentric" was perhaps too gentle a word—the kind of charitable understatement that people employ when they are trying to reconcile the man they thought they knew with the monster he had revealed himself to be. For eccentricity suggests harmless oddity, the sort of mild strangeness that makes for amusing dinner party conversation rather than 48 days of community-wide terror.

What they meant, though they may not have possessed the words to articulate it precisely, was that Eric Matthew Frein had always carried about him the peculiar quality of a man slightly out of step with the world around him. Not dramatically so—not in the obvious way of the neighborhood madman or the raving street-corner prophet—but with the subtler disconnection of someone who viewed his fellow human beings from a distance, as if they were specimens in a laboratory rather than neighbors sharing the same patch of earth.

The conversations that followed his capture possessed a quality common to such revelations: the slow, painful process by which ordinary people attempt to reconstruct their understanding of someone they had lived alongside for years. They found themselves examining every mundane interaction through the lens of hindsight, searching for clues they might have missed, signs they should have recognized, warnings they ought to have heeded.

"He kept to himself," they would say, though this phrase—so common in the aftermath of such revelations—barely scratched the surface of what they had observed. Keeping to oneself can suggest simple introversion or a preference for privacy. What they had witnessed was something more deliberate: a man who seemed to have constructed invisible walls around himself, who participated in the basic social interactions of neighborhood life without ever quite belonging to them.

There were, they recalled, the long periods when he would disappear entirely—vanishing for days or weeks at a time, presumably engaged in his elaborate war games and military reenactments. During these absences, the Frein property in Canadensis would take on the hollow quality of a house temporarily abandoned, as if its occupant had simply stepped out of ordinary life and into some parallel existence where different rules applied.

When he did appear, it was often in the context of his obsessions. Neighbors remembered seeing him in military surplus clothing, carrying equipment that seemed excessive for weekend recreational activities. At the time, they had perhaps attributed this to the harmless enthusiasm of a hobbyist—the sort of man who becomes completely absorbed in model trains or Civil War memorabilia. Only later would they understand that what they had witnessed was not a hobby but preparation.

The children of the neighborhood, possessed of that peculiar intuition that allows them to sense what adults often miss, had always given Eric Frein a wide berth. Not because he had ever threatened them or behaved inappropriately, but because something in his demeanor suggested a man who inhabited a different world from the one they knew—a world where children's games and suburban concerns held no meaning.

In the days following his capture, those same neighbors would tell reporters that they felt like "prisoners in our own homes" during the manhunt, a phrase that captured not just the immediate terror of those 48 days but also, perhaps, the retrospective understanding that they had been living adjacent to danger for far longer than they had realized.

The most haunting aspect of their recollections was not what they remembered, but what they realized they had never known. For all the years Eric Frein had lived among them, he had remained fundamentally unknowable, a man who had mastered the art of existing in plain sight while revealing nothing essential about himself. He was, in the truest sense, a stranger who happened to live nearby, someone who shared their geography without ever sharing their humanity.

In the end, the neighbors' descriptions of Eric Frein painted the portrait of a man who had been practicing invisibility long before he disappeared into the Pennsylvania woods— someone who had learned to move through the world without leaving the sort of impression that would make him truly memorable. It was, perhaps, the perfect preparation for a man who would one day need to vanish entirely.

Why September 12? Why that specific, humid Friday, when the moon was waning and the weekend beckoned? The calendar of the mass killer is rarely a random lottery; it is almost always a schedule dictated by a private, invisible crisis.

We know the preparation—the years of hoarding, the research into ballistics, the slow calcification of his heart. But we miss the precipitating event, the single grain of sand that finally tips the scale. In the days leading up to the ambush, a peculiar calm had descended upon Eric Frein. His mother, Debbie, noted it with a mother's anxious relief: he had "snapped out" of his long, sullen moodiness. He was chatty. He was helpful. He was "normal."

To the uninitiated, this looked like recovery. To the student of the suicidal mind, it looked like resolution. It is a phenomenon well known to psychiatrists: the euphoric peace that settles upon a person once the terrible decision has been made. The agonizing choice is over; only the execution remains.

But what triggered the decision? What happened in the quiet, desperate ecosystem of the Frein household in the first week of September 2014? Was there a quarrel over money? A threat of eviction? A final, humiliating realization that the summer was ending and his life remained exactly where it had been the year before, and the year before that? Or was it something smaller, a slight so microscopic that only a narcissist would feel its sting? A glance from a girl who looked through him? A rejection letter?

The mystery of that final week is the black box of the Frein case. We have the flight data recorder of his actions, but the cockpit voice recorder, the internal monologue of the final countdown, remains erased. We are left only with the silence of the woods and the terrifying possibility that the trigger was nothing more than the intolerable weight of his own insignificance, finally reaching critical mass.

BEHIND THE WARRIORS

In the humid, watchful silence of the Pocono brush, there were men who carried neither rifles nor the heavy, metallic burden of justice, yet they walked the same jagged miles as the FBI and the Customs and Border Patrol agents. These were the paramedics, the silent custodians of the living, moving through the undergrowth like ghosts in high-visibility shadows.

To the uninitiated, the distinction between a paramedic and an emergency medical technician—the humble EMT— might seem a trifle, a matter of mere nomenclature. But in the theater of a manhunt, the difference is as vast as the distance between a man who can patch a leak and a man who can rewire the heart. The EMT is a technician of the immediate: a steady hand to bind a wound, a sentinel of oxygen and basic rhythm, trained in the essential, frantic grammar of the first response. They are the infantry of medicine, capable and vital, yet bound by the limits of the non-invasive.

A paramedic, however, is a clinician of the woods. They are the ones who carry the chemistry of survival in their kits— the narcotics to dull a scream, the needles to pierce a failing vein, the plastic tubes to keep a windpipe from collapsing into a final, suffocating silence. While the EMT waits for the ambulance, the paramedic is the hospital, a portable sanctuary of advanced life support capable of performing the delicate, invasive sorcery of intubation or chest decompression while a sniper's potential shadow lengthens across the ferns.

During those 48 days of the hunt for Eric Frein, these medics were "embedded," a military term for a civilian sacrifice. They stood behind the federal agents in the stagnant air of the Birchwood-Pocono Airpark, their pulses thrumming not with the hunt, but with the heavy, clinical anticipation of the "golden hour"—that fleeting window where a life, shattered by a .308-caliber round, might still be caught and held. They were there for the troopers, for the agents, and even, should the need arise, for the fugitive himself—because the paramedic's code is a cold and objective thing, indifferent to the moral weight of the flesh it must preserve. They waited in the damp October rot, their fingers tracing the outlines of laryngoscopes and vials, ready to mend the very holes the men with rifles were so meticulously trying to avoid making in themselves.

THE FREIN PERSONA

THE SIEGE OF SENECA LANE

While the son played hide-and-seek in the vast, indifferent woods, the parents were trapped in a fishbowl of their own making. The house on Seneca Lane in Canadesis, a modest suburban structure with vinyl siding and a manicured lawn, had become the most watched building in America.

The siege here was not military, but psychological. The media vans camped on the lawn like a flock of metallic vultures, their satellite dishes turned upward, waiting for a signal. Cameras with telephoto lenses were trained on the windows, hoping to catch a glimpse of the monsters who had raised a monster.

Inside, Eugene and Debbie Frein moved through the rooms with the curtains drawn, living in a perpetual twilight. The phone rang with a relentless, shrill persistence. Sometimes it was the FBI, polite but unyielding; sometimes it was a reporter, hungry for a quote; sometimes it was the silence of a crank caller, breathing hate down the line.

They hoped it was Eric. They feared it was the coroner.

The dynamic between husband and wife was a wire pulled to the breaking point. Debbie, the mother, lived in the suffocating fog of denial. How could her boy—her quiet, awkward boy who loved history—be the face on the "Wanted" posters? She moved through the house like a ghost, touching his things, trying to reconcile the child she had nursed with the sniper the world described.

But the rot was deeper. It sat at the head of the dinner table.

Eugene Frein, a retired U.S. Army major, had built a cathedral of lies, and his son had been its most devout worshipper. The FBI agents, in their quiet, probing interviews, began to dismantle the mythology. They found that the war stories

Eugene told—the tales of combat in Vietnam, the secret missions, the heroism—were largely fabrications, the stolen valor of a man who needed to be more than he was.

Imagine the dinner table of Eric's youth: the father spinning these golden threads of fiction, the son catching them and weaving them into a worldview. The father's disdain for the police, his complaints about the government, his posturing as a warrior—it was a virus passed from father to son, incubating over decades. Now, trapped in the house, Eugene had to look at the empty seat and know that his lies had armed his son just as surely as if he had bought the rifle himself.

To understand the son, one must first exhume the father. Eugene Frein was a man constructed of bluster and fabrication. He was the architect of the family's reality, building a cathedral of war out of straw and lies. He spun golden threads of fiction—tales of Vietnam snipers, of secret missions in the jungle, of a heroism that existed only in the vapor of his own whiskey-soaked breath.

He was a microbiologist who had never seen the jungle, a major of the reserves who yearned for the blood-rust of the battlefield but settled for the safety of the laboratory. But to the boy, wide-eyed and quiet, the lies were gospel. Eric Frein did not inherit a war; he inherited a phantom. He grew up in the shadow of a giant who cast no reflection, nourished on the poison of stolen valor.

The father taught the son that the world was a battlefield, that the police were the enemy, and that violence was the only language the State understood. And so, when the son finally picked up the rifle and walked into the woods, he was not merely acting out a fantasy; he was trying to become the man his father had only pretended to be, unaware that he was marching to war under a flag that had never truly flown.

THE DUALITY OF FREIN

Eric Frein's deep psychological landscape was characterized by a profound, disturbing duality, a terrain where deep-seated personal inadequacies were transformed into a motive for calculated murder. The experts found him to be a methodical intelligence who was neither a raging madman nor a simple psychopath, but a "mission-oriented killer" who approached violence with a chilling, clinical detachment. His core delusion was a narcissistic-grandiose conviction that his "solitary, violent act" would be the "spark to ignite fire" in a nation gone astray. This delusion was an escape from his own personal failure, which he reframed as persecution by a corrupt government, thus transforming his "personal inadequacy" into an "ideological framework" for violence.

His character was defined by his rigorous performance of the soldier's role: he was a man of "uncommon quietness" whose social isolation was replaced by an obsessive commitment to martial ritual and military reenactment. This commitment evolved into a "psychological bridge to actual violence." He maintained a frightening "clinical separation" from the moral enormity of his acts, even stating that his victim "knew the risks" when he put on the uniform. His disguising of hate as ideology created a man of "ordinary intelligence and extraordinary hatred."

Frein's act of terrorism provoked an immediate, comprehensive deployment of State power, turning his personal rebellion into a demonstration of the State's unyielding authority. The search, led by Lieutenant Colonel George Bivens, became one of the most extensive fugitive searches in Pennsylvania's recent memory, involving up to 1,000 officers from multiple federal and state agencies and costing nearly $12 million.

The operation utilized sophisticated methods, including thermal imaging, tracking dogs Frein countered with "water crossings," armored BearCat vehicles, and even a "$180,000 tethered helium balloon," a mechanical observer that provided continuous surveillance.

Frein, however, treated the evasion as a "game," demonstrating an "almost artistic mastery of the ancient craft of disappearing" by leaving behind "empty packs of Serbian cigarettes and soiled diapers." His own journal documented his struggle, revealing a "curious mixture of pride and resignation," grappling with the failure of his expected revolution.

The 48-day flight ended "without incident" on October 30, 2014, at the abandoned Birchwood-Pocono Airpark near Tannersville. In a final, chilling act of "poetic justice," arresting officers placed Corporal Dickson's handcuffs on Frein's wrists and transported him back to the Blooming Grove barracks in the dead trooper's squad car.

The jury's path to the death sentence was paved by their absolute acceptance of all aggravating circumstances and zero mitigating circumstances, a final verdict that legally mandated execution.

The foundational aggravator was the murder of a peace officer committed during the perpetration of multiple high-level felonies, including the attempted murder and assault of a law enforcement officer (Trooper Alex Douglass), terrorism, weapons of mass destruction, and the knowing creation of a grave risk of death to additional persons, including PCO Nicole Palmer.

The simultaneous conviction for the other murder charge further cemented the verdict. The sheer weight of these factors ensured that the defense's entire mitigating case—

all 30 points—was officially discarded, removing the "foundation for granting mercy."

The legal challenges were defined by the tension between morality and procedure. Attorney William Ruzzo made a final, desperate motion to have the jury consider the "impact of an execution on the victim's [Frein's] family," an attempt to introduce mercy that was ultimately denied as being squarely against Pennsylvania case law.

Similarly, the Court denied Ruzzo's request, based on the *Tennard v. Dretke* case, to instruct the jury that they did not need to establish a "nexus" (a connection) between Frein's mental issues and the crime.

Crucially, the Court neutralized the defense's attempt to argue mental health by issuing a curative instruction, ordering the jury to disregard Debbie Frein's outbursts that her son was "delusional" and suffered from a "frontal lobe" injury. This act ensured the jury focused on the facts, not the unsupported emotional theories.

Finally, Eric Frein is now confined in a Pennsylvania correctional facility, SCI Phoenix, a population where death row itself is often less a swift sentence than a "condition" of protracted waiting. The death penalty machinery in Pennsylvania has largely rusted into dormancy, with a gubernatorial moratorium having suspended executions since 2015. Frein's existence is now a sentence of "slow tumbling of days in the humid blankness of cells," though with reforms granting "forty-two and a half hours out" per week in communal air—a life that is "not freedom at all, but a widening of the cell." The core irony remains: the man who attempted to incite a revolution is now a "ghost in the machinery," his life defined by the system he sought to dismantle.

THE ARCHITECTURE
OF A KILLER'S MIND

In the months that followed Eric Matthew Frein's capture, psychiatrists and criminal psychologists attempted to construct a blueprint of the mind that had conceived such calculated violence. What they discovered was not the raging psychopath of popular imagination, but something far more disturbing: a man of methodical intelligence who had transformed hatred into a kind of art form, who had approached murder with the same systematic precision that other men brought to stamp collecting or model railroading.

Dr. Katherine Ramsland, the forensic psychologist who spent 47 hours interviewing Frein in the months following his arrest, would later describe the experience as one of the most unsettling of her career. She had interviewed serial killers and mass murderers, had spent decades mapping the geography of criminal minds, yet there was something about Frein's calm self-possession that troubled her sleep for months afterward.

"He spoke of killing Corporal Dickson the way another man might describe changing a tire," she would write in her preliminary report. "There was no passion, no rage, no evidence of the emotional turmoil we typically associate with violent crime. It was as if he were recounting a technical procedure he had performed successfully."

The psychological portrait that emerged from these sessions revealed a man who had spent years nurturing his grievances like rare orchids, tending them with obsessive care until they bloomed into something monstrous. Frein's childhood, by all accounts, had been unremarkable—middle-class suburban comfort, two parents who worked steady jobs, a younger sister who would grow up to become a nurse. There had been no obvious trauma, no precipitating event that could explain the transformation of Eric Frein from suburban teenager to domestic terrorist.

Instead, what the psychiatrists found was a mind that had constructed an elaborate mythology around its own grievances, a personal narrative in which Eric Frein was simultaneously victim and hero, oppressed citizen and righteous warrior. His anti-government ideology was not born of philosophical conviction but of personal inadequacy transformed into political anger. He had failed at most things he had attempted—college, relationships, careers— and had gradually come to blame his failures not on his own limitations, but on a corrupt system that had somehow conspired against him.

The modification of his appearance in the months before the shooting—the Mohawk haircut, the physical conditioning, the adoption of military surplus clothing—represented what Dr. Ramsland termed "the external manifestation of an internal transformation." Frein was not merely planning a crime; he was creating a character, fashioning himself into the kind of man who could commit such acts. It was method acting taken to its most extreme and dangerous conclusion.

His research into police tactics and manhunt procedures, documented through forensic analysis of his computer hard drives, revealed a mind that approached violence with scientific methodology. For more than two years before the shooting, Frein had studied law enforcement techniques with the dedication of a graduate student. He had researched supply caching methods, counter-surveillance techniques, and the psychological factors that had led to the capture of other fugitives. This was not the impulsive violence of a man pushed beyond his limits, but the calculated preparation of someone who had transformed killing into a technical problem to be solved.

The journals he kept during his 48 days as a fugitive provided perhaps the most chilling insight into his psychological state. Written in a careful, almost delicate handwriting, these entries revealed a man who was simultaneously surprised by his own endurance and increasingly aware of the inevitable conclusion to his woodland odyssey. There was a curious mixture of pride and resignation in these writings, as if he were congratulating himself on his woodcraft while preparing for the martyrdom he seemed to believe awaited him.

"Day 23," read one entry discovered by investigators. "Nearly stepped on a patrol this morning. Could have taken two of them easily but held my fire. This is not about numbers. The message has been sent." The clinical detachment of the prose was remarkable—the same tone one might use to describe a successful fishing expedition or a particularly challenging crossword puzzle.

Dr. James Garbarino, the criminal psychologist who served as consultant to the prosecution, would later testify that Frein exhibited many characteristics of what researchers term the "mission-oriented killer"—an individual who views violence not as an expression of personal pathology but as a necessary tool for achieving ideological goals. Such individuals, Garbarino explained, often display above-average intelligence, meticulous planning abilities, and a frightening capacity for compartmentalization that allows them to separate their violent acts from their everyday emotional responses.

"Mr. Frein did not kill Corporal Dickson in a moment of passion or psychotic break," Garbarino testified during the penalty phase of the trial. "He killed him because he had decided that killing police officers was necessary to advance his anti-government agenda. The crime was not a symptom of mental illness but the logical conclusion of a belief system that had transformed other human beings into symbols rather than people."

Perhaps most disturbing was Frein's apparent lack of empathy for his victims. When Dr. Ramsland pressed him about the impact of his actions on Corporal Dickson's family, Frein's response was telling: "He chose to put on that uniform. He knew the risks." It was as if the badge had somehow stripped Dickson of his humanity, transforming him from husband and father into legitimate military target. This dehumanization, the psychiatrists noted, was essential to Frein's ability to function normally before and after the shooting—he could compartmentalize violence by convincing himself that his victims were not truly human.

The question that haunted the psychological evaluations was perhaps unanswerable: how does a suburban, middle-class American transform himself into a domestic terrorist? The answer, according to the experts, lay not in any single dramatic event but in the gradual accumulation of disappointments and resentments that eventually crystallized into something approaching religious conviction. Eric Frein had created a mythology in which his personal failures became evidence of systematic oppression, in which violence became not only justified but morally necessary.

When the interviews were concluded and the reports filed, the psychological portrait of Eric Matthew Frein that emerged was that of a man who had methodically erased his own humanity in service of an ideology that existed primarily in his own mind. He was neither madman nor monster, but something perhaps more frightening: a man of ordinary intelligence and extraordinary hatred who had discovered that the distance between suburban discontentment and calculated murder was shorter than most people dared to imagine.

Eric Frein's psychological landscape was a terrain not unlike those thick, shadowed woods he knew so well—dense, tangled, and haunted by old ghosts and private battles, shaped and patrolled by silent laws of his own making. If one were to walk its shaded paths, one would find not the vestiges of mere solitude, but the obsessive geometry of a mind forever drawn to the martial, to ritual, to the idea and image of war itself.

He was a man of uncommon quietness, the kind whose presence presses inward, not outward. In youth, he proved a quick study in the order of things: the merit badge, the cold authority of the rifle, the sharp cut of a uniform. Yet even then, the line between preparation and obsession—between hobby and compulsion—seemed perilously thin. His rooms amassed the detritus of old conflicts: surplus boots, Balkan cigarettes, the dulled brass of a foreign insignia polished with reverence. These were not trophies but signifiers—a filial longing for honor grafted with a current of alienation.

At the root of Frein's disquiet lay a legacy: the shadow of his father, a retired major whose stories bore the legend of heroism and whose standards, it seemed, receded further the nearer Frein drew to them. The old man's tales did not inspire emulation so much as they did a kind of urgent, weary envy; the boy who could not measure up became the man who stockpiled resentment, its weight multiplying with every retelling.

Those who knew Frein best, or tried to, described a transformation that grew more pronounced with years—he drifted from the camaraderie of reenactors into a brooding remove, his devotion to details no longer merely scholarly, but absolute. He saw himself less as an actor in someone else's script than as the rare soul living out the unfinished story of a nation gone astray. The boundaries between simulation and intent, between fantasy and reality, dissolved:

in the dust and gun oil, he rehearsed for a battle only he could see.

If his was, at times, a cold manner—detached, unemotional in the recounting of his deeds—it sprang not from stupidity or native cruelty, but from a calculated resolve. Law enforcement, when they hunted him as he slipped through the rocky underbrush, believed he regarded it all as a grim sport. He migrated through shadows, shorn his hair to a Mohawk, left behind the small, mocking tokens meant to bait those who followed—acts not of senseless violence, but of method and message, a kind of strategic artifice.

The words he left behind, oddly gentle in their looping hand, made plain the manifesto of his heart. He chronicled his grievances, told of a nation ruined by "depressing changes," evangelized the necessity of revolution, believed, with an almost mystical certainty, that violence might reignite the old, essential fires—and that he, Eric Frein, would be the spark.

Yet to those who dared peer inward—and few could, or cared to—the true center of his storm was lonelier still. He was, in the end, a man hunting for meaning in the borderlands between fiction and fact, anger and inadequacy, yearning for the approval he could neither claim nor refuse. Where others recalled him as an Eagle Scout, a young man adrift, the reality was starker: he did not merely adapt to the logic of war; he was consumed by it. The lines between dress and intent, memory and prophecy, narrowed until the future he dreaded was the only one he could inhabit.

The ambush itself, cold and patient, was not an eruption but a culmination—the hard logic of grievance brought to fatal expression. There, on the gravel at the edge of the treeline, he stepped fully into the role he had rehearsed for so long: soldier, sniper, architect of disorder and despair. Held at gunpoint and through crosshairs, the world could finally see him as he saw himself: not a madman, perhaps, but a product of old wounds and older stories, of obsessions kept banked like coals until the night returned to chaos.

Like so many before him who had vanished into the dense heart of their own making, Frein did not seek carnage for its own sake. He sought, however destructively, a sense of belonging, a redemption none could grant, and the chilling thrill of becoming, for an instant at least, the ghost at the nation's crossroads—half relic, half warning, entirely alone.

To look upon the face of Eric Matthew Frein was to confront a peculiar stillness, as though the man himself were listening for something, some distant echo that only he could hear. His eyes carried the strange composure of someone who had long rehearsed the act of being alone, who found in isolation not punishment but a private kind of order. In the brooding folds of the Poconos, where mist settled like old memory and each shadow seemed eager to keep a secret, Frein did not merely vanish; he became the whisper that pursued him. There, in the damp breath of the forest, his thoughts darkened and clarified until cruelty itself took on the purity of a plan.

He was a child of the suburbs, a "reenactor" by trade and by temperament. There was in him a distinct yearning for a grandiosity that life had seen fit to deny him. He lived within the cramped quarters of his parents' home, yet his mind wandered through the battlefields of Eastern Europe, draped in the heavy wool of a Serbian paramilitary uniform.[1]

The psychological soil from which such a man grows is often tilled with perceived grievance and a hunger for

---

1. FBI Case Study: *The Radicalization of Eric Frein* (2015). Documents his deep immersion in Eastern European paramilitary culture as a precursor to his anti-government shift.

significance.[2] In Frein, we see the "lone wolf" who is never truly alone, but rather accompanied by a legion of imagined heroes and historical ghosts. He did not see the Pennsylvania State Police as men with families and fatigue; he saw them as symbols—the "blue-clad oppressors" necessary for the completion of his personal myth.[3]

The "warning signs" in the Frein case were not shouts but whispers—the soft snapping of twigs before the predator reveals itself. Those who study the dark mechanics of the radicalized mind speak of a "pathway to violence," a series of steps taken with agonizing deliberation.[4]

For Frein, this began with the rehearsal of the self. His obsession with military reenactment was not a mere hobby but a "dry run" for his psyche; he was practicing the coldness required to pull a trigger, dressing the part until the heavy costume became the skin itself. This evolved into a quiet stockpiling of hate long before the first shot echoed at the Blooming Grove barracks. He gathered his tools—the .308 rifle, the pipe bombs, the meticulously kept journals—with the focused diligence of an artisan, all while maintaining the placid, unremarkable exterior of a quiet neighbor.

Finally, there was the leakage of intent, that digital and paper trail where the secret of his perceived greatness could no longer be contained. He left behind a manifesto declaring that "tension is needed" to spark a revolution, a classic

---

2. Kruglanski, A.W. (2014). *The Psychology of Radicalization.* Discusses the "quest for significance" as a primary driver for extremist violence.

3. Pennsylvania State Police Records (2014-2017). *Commonwealth v. Eric Frein.* Detailed evidence of his long-term planning and the survivalist manifestos found in the woods.

4. Meloy, J.R. & O'Toole, M.E. (2001). *The Concept of Leakage in Threat Assessment.* Defines the "warning signs" when a subject communicates intent to a third party.

hallmark of the extremist who feels compelled to broadcast his internal war to an uncomprehending world.[5]

On that humid September night in 2014, the transition from "predisposition" to "action" was finalized. In the mind of the domestic terrorist, the target is never a human being; it is an "abstraction." By dehumanizing Corporal Bryon Dickson and Trooper Alex Douglass, Frein allowed himself the "moral disengagement" necessary to fire from the darkness.

The 48-day manhunt that followed was the climax of his play. He lived on canned tuna fish and cigarettes, watching the massive machinery of the State grind through the brush, likely savoring the fact that for once, the world was forced to look at him.

REFLECTIONS FROM THE FLIGHT

Deep in the Pennsylvania woods, while a thousand law enforcement officers combed the forest floor for any trace of his passage, Eric Matthew Frein found time to write. These were not the frantic scribblings of a desperate fugitive, but careful, deliberate entries in what would become his most damning evidence—a journal that revealed the interior landscape of a man who had convinced himself he was making history rather than running from it.

The journal, discovered among his belongings and later read aloud in a Pike County courtroom, offered a window into the mind of someone who had transformed his flight from justice into an elaborate performance piece, complete

5. Department of Homeland Security (DHS): *Analysis of Domestic Violent Extremism* (2021). Notes the use of personal journals as a tool for radicalization and moral justification.

with philosophical justifications and historical pretensions. "What I have done has not been done before, and it felt like it was worth a try," Frein had scrawled during his weeks of evasion, words that captured both his grandiose self-perception and his fundamental misunderstanding of his place in the world.

Here was a man writing his own mythology even as he lived it, transforming his desperate flight through the Pocono Mountains into what he imagined was a principled stand against tyranny. The entries revealed someone who had never quite grasped the difference between the elaborate war games he had played for years and the very real consequences of actual violence. In his mind, apparently, he had graduated from weekend warrior to genuine revolutionary, though the revolution existed primarily in his imagination.

Perhaps most telling was what the journal revealed about Frein's relationship to time during those 48 days. The alleged cop killer appeared surprised that the weeks-long manhunt went on as long as it did, suggesting a man who had planned his dramatic gesture but had not entirely thought through its aftermath. The meticulous preparation that had gone into the ambush itself—the careful reconnaissance, the selection of weapons, the choice of target—seemed to give way to improvisation once the reality of life as a hunted fugitive set in.

The writings painted a picture of a man caught between personas: part political philosopher, part survivalist hero, part frightened fugitive. He had entered the woods believing himself to be a catalyst for change, someone whose actions would awaken his fellow Americans to the necessity of revolution. Instead, he found himself engaged in the most basic struggle of all—the simple animal need to avoid capture, to find food and shelter, to survive another day.

One can imagine him during those long nights in his improvised shelters, writing by whatever dim light he dared risk, trying to make sense of a situation that had spiraled far beyond his control. The journal entries suggest a man grappling with the growing realization that his grand gesture had produced not political awakening but simply grief and an extensive manhunt. The revolution he had hoped to spark had failed to materialize, leaving him alone in the wilderness with nothing but his words and his rapidly diminishing supplies.

The act of writing seemed to serve as a kind of psychological anchor for Frein during his weeks of evasion. In a world that had been reduced to its most elemental components—food, water, shelter, the constant fear of discovery—the journal represented his attempt to maintain some connection to his identity as something more than a common criminal. Through writing, he could preserve the fiction that he remained a political actor rather than simply a man running for his life.

Yet the very existence of the journal also revealed something else. Despite all his preparation, despite his elaborate counter-tracking techniques and survival skills, Eric Frein had never truly believed he would remain free indefinitely. The act of documenting his thoughts and experiences suggested someone who understood, perhaps unconsciously, that these writings might someday serve as his final statement—the last communication from a man who had mistaken terrorism for revolution and found himself trapped in the consequences of that confusion.

The journal concluded not with triumph or defiant proclamation, but with the gradual recognition that the world had not responded to his actions as he had hoped. Instead of awakening his countrymen to the necessity of change, he had simply added his name to the long list of those who had chosen violence over persuasion and found themselves, in the end, alone with their words and their regrets in the unforgiving wilderness of their own making.

Consider the plight of Mr. James Tully, a local pedestrian of unfortunate aspect, whose daily constitutionals to his place of employment became a gauntlet of suspicion. Mr. Tully, by a cruel trick of genetics, bore a resemblance to the phantom in the woods that was striking enough to stop traffic—specifically, the traffic of law enforcement. More than 20 times, the lights flashed and the questions came. On one particularly jagged afternoon, the encounter shed its veneer of procedure. Mr. Tully found himself pressed into the dirt, the cold eye of a rifle bore fixed upon him, rising later with bruised ribs and a shaken faith in the safety of the innocent. It was a cruelty that the community, in a burst of collective conscience, sought to remedy. They passed the hat, gathering funds not for a reward but for a sedan, ensuring that Mr. Tully might drive through the "Frein Zone" encased in steel, insulated from the perils of his own face.

The woods, it seemed, were being used not merely as a hiding place, but as a message board. The police, combing the underbrush with the grim determination of archeologists, unearthed a trail that suggested a mockery of the pursuit, with the decrepit remnants of a man who left a trail of bodily refuge and tantalizing cultural clues.

As the weeks wore on and Frein ghosted through the terrain, utilizing the creeks and the damp earth to confound the nose of the bloodhound, a voice from his past offered a theory that bordered on the theatrical. A former comrade from the Red Alliance, that fraternity of grown men who dress in the costumes of war, suggested that Eric was no longer playing a game of his own invention, but was stepping into a script written by Hollywood. He was, the friend posited, reenacting *First Blood*, casting himself as John Rambo, the misunderstood warrior pitting his woodcraft against the heavy, clumsy machinery of the State.

But if this was a movie, the opening scene had been a disaster of unscripted incompetence. The escape, the grand withdrawal into the wilderness, had faltered at the very start. Driving his Jeep Cherokee through the black Pennsylvania night with his headlights extinguished—a tactic of stealth that proved his undoing—Frein failed to negotiate the road. The vehicle, carrying the tools of his revolution, pitched into a swampy retention pond mere miles from the scene of the crime. He was forced to abandon the Jeep to the mud, fleeing on foot and leaving behind a treasure trove of identity: his driver's license, shell casings, the very paper trail that would strip him of his anonymity before the sun rose.

Perhaps the most chilling artifact pulled from the forest floor was found in a trash bag at a campsite hastily vacated. It was a handwritten journal, a diary of the damnation he had wrought. In prose that was terrifyingly flat, he recounted the ambush. He described the falling of Corporal Dickson not with horror, but with a detached curiosity, noting how the man went "still and quiet." He expressed a technician's surprise at the speed of the event, the suddenness with which a life could be extinguished. It was a window into a mind where empathy had been surgically removed, leaving only a cold, observational silence.

THE HANGAR

On October 30, 2014, Deputy U.S. Marshal Scott Malkowski and his 11-man Special Operations Group team were conducting another methodical sweep of their assigned grid, this one encompassing an abandoned airstrip and resort near Tannersville. The Birchwood-Pocono Airpark was one of countless forgotten remnants of the region's more prosperous past, but it carried within its decaying structures the entire arc of American dreams and their inevitable dissolution.

Birchwood had once embodied the romantic excess of the Pocono Mountains' golden age as the "Honeymoon Capital of the World." Built in the early 1960s by Wally Hoffman Jr., a Pan Am pilot and founder of Pocono Airlines, the resort represented the intersection of aviation glamor and romantic escapism that defined an era. The complex had been designed as a couples-only retreat, "like a cruise on land," complete with private cottages scattered around ornamental ponds, winding foot paths that meandered through carefully manicured grounds, an indoor swimming pool, bowling alley, cross-country ski area, roller skating rink, and nightly entertainment that promised to keep honeymooners enchanted throughout their stay.

The airstrip itself was Hoffman's masterstroke—a 2,800-foot runway that allowed wealthy couples to fly directly to their romantic getaway, bypassing the increasingly congested highways that brought less affluent visitors to the region. Small aircraft would taxi up to the resort's buildings, their passengers stepping directly from private planes into a world of manufactured romance. It was the kind of vertical integration that marked the most successful resort operators of the era, a seamless blend of transportation and hospitality that catered to America's post-war prosperity.

But by the late 1990s, the dream had soured. Like so many Pocono resorts, Birchwood fell victim to changing tastes, increased competition from more exotic destinations, and the inevitable mortality of its founding generation. The airstrip closed in 1998, its runway gradually surrendering to weeds and weather. The resort buildings, once alive with the laughter of newlyweds, stood empty, their windows broken by vandals and time, their roofs sagging under the weight of accumulated snow and neglect.

When Eric Frein stumbled upon this abandoned paradise during his weeks as a fugitive, he found a landscape that perfectly matched his own psychological terrain—a place where American optimism had curdled into decay, where the symbols of prosperity had become monuments to failure. The resort's scattered buildings provided numerous hiding places, while the abandoned runway offered clear sight lines in all directions. It was, in its way, the perfect metaphor for Frein's own journey from suburban comfort to criminal infamy.

The hangar where Frein was ultimately captured stood at the far end of the runway, a cavernous metal structure that had once sheltered the aircraft of weekend romantics. By 2014, it had become a warehouse of forgotten dreams, rusted maintenance equipment, discarded furniture, the detritus of a business that had simply stopped one day and never resumed. Inside this hollow shell, investigators would later discover the pathetic inventory of Frein's fugitive existence: contact lenses, first aid supplies, toilet paper, a book of the New Testament, a religious plaque, and even DVDs—the survival cache of a man who had traded his anti-government ideology for the basic human need for shelter and entertainment.

It was the kind of routine search that had been conducted hundreds of times over the previous weeks, the sort of painstaking work that defines modern manhunts. Malkowski spotted movement first—a figure emerging from the treeline toward the abandoned hangar. Hidden by tall grass that had grown wild in the absence of maintenance, the marshal moved with the stealth that his training had ingrained, closing the distance while Frein remained unaware of his approach. The airfield's open expanse, once designed to provide aircraft with clear landing approaches, now worked against the fugitive, offering him nowhere to hide once he had been spotted.

When recognition dawned, Malkowski's training took over. "Suspect," he whispered to his team, then called out his identification and ordered Frein to the ground. The man who had terrorized a region for nearly seven weeks, who had evaded thermal imaging and search dogs and surveillance balloons, who had played cat-and-mouse with a thousand officers, simply surrendered. He was armed with a sniper rifle and knives, the tools of his deadly trade, but the fight had gone out of him. No shots were fired. No dramatic chase ensued across the cracked tarmac of the abandoned runway. When he appeared in court the following day, Frein looked thin and haggard from his weeks in the wilderness, with a cut on his nose and abrasions on his forehead, his left cheek swollen from his time living rough in the Pennsylvania woods.

As Malkowski later recalled, "He had nowhere to go. There is nothing he could've done." Perhaps Frein recognized that his particular brand of performance art had reached its natural conclusion, or perhaps the 48 days in the wilderness had finally broken something essential in his resistance.

The symbolism of the capture location was inescapable—a man whose ideology had been built around the supposed corruption of American institutions, captured in the ruins of American enterprise. Birchwood-Pocono Airpark represented everything that Frein's survivalist philosophy claimed to reject: corporate excess, consumer culture, the commodification of human emotion. Yet in the end, it was these abandoned symbols of capitalism that provided him shelter, and it was among their ruins that his revolution came to its inglorious conclusion.

In a gesture that spoke to the deep personal nature of the crime, arresting officers placed Corporal Dickson's handcuffs on Frein's wrists and transported him back to the Blooming Grove barracks in the dead trooper's squad car. It was theater of a different sort—the kind of poetic justice that real life occasionally provides but fiction rarely dares to attempt.

It was an act of fate that the marshals would capture the Pennsylvania state trooper's prey. The marshals happened to be assigned a grid area to search that day, another methodical tactic in what became hundreds or thousands of decisions during the search for Frein. And one that no doubt sat poorly with the state police.

The manhunt that finally claimed him lasted until "the night of October 30, 2014, at an abandoned airport," bringing to a close what had become the most extensive fugitive search in Pennsylvania's recent memory. One imagines that final moment—the man who had spent weeks as a phantom suddenly corporeal again, blinking in the harsh glare of police flashlights like an actor caught between scenes, the spell of his performance finally broken.

In the end, Eric Frein's greatest achievement may have been transforming himself into exactly what his years of reenactment had prepared him to be: a soldier in a war of his own making, fighting an enemy that existed primarily in his mind, using skills learned in the service of fantasy to wage a very real battle against a world that had never declared war on him at all.

Frein emerged from the quiet capture with a bloodied face, attributed by law enforcement to his struggle during the capture process. But rumors swirled of a head-stomp while he was being restrained, according to local police officers.

His booking photo and perp walk reflected the freshness of the injuries.

Beneath a bruised October sky, dusk flinched over the melancholy expanse of Birchwood-Pocono Airpark, the bones of abandoned hangars shouldering years of silence. Lawmen, boots grinding against cold asphalt, fanned out—a phalanx not of raw vengeance, but of procedural steel, exhaustion rendering everyone brittle as autumn grass. Somewhere between memory and rumor, the fugitive became myth: Eric Frein, tall, hollow-eyed, the boy all grown into trouble and terror, drifting thin as mist, hunted for 48 days amid black pine barrens and unforgiving stone.

When the marshals came upon him, Frein did not run. Gone were the games played in the woods—no more cat-and-mouse, no more camouflage. Ordered down, he complied, knees to gravel, hands raised in mute surrender, his defeat naked and profound, the drama of it broadcast by the abrupt hush of the men who found him. Yet, as with any tale that stains history, what happened next is a braid of method, myth, and midnight rumor. To secure him—so the official account runs—one marshal acted on training, pressing Frein face down into the unyielding runway, asphalt rough against the bridge of his nose, cheekbones grinding into stone. "Never have a fugitive look at you," they had learned. And so, his face became a map of oozing scrapes and bruises, his brow bloodied, eye rim darkening already.

But the bruises, the swollen nose, the unspoken chill added another note—a whisper that what was done to Frein on that cracked runway bled the color of retribution. It is said—not in court, but in hushed voices in barrooms and on porches—that the pressure of the lawman's hand on Frein's scalp was more than precaution, more than protocol. That perhaps, pressed there under the cold gaze of justice, it was vengeance for Corporal Dickson, who lay buried in late September earth, for the wound that haunted Trooper Douglass through all those weeks of rage and worry. One marshal said simply, "We meant business. Especially when he killed a fellow officer."

Fact intertwines with feeling in moments like these. The world can only watch as the perpetrator, for whose deeds there is no forgetting, bleeds beneath the hands of law and rumor both. Eric Frein is cuffed, not with new steel, but with Dickson's own cuffs. He rides in Dickson's car, along the road where blood was first drawn, past shuttered houses straining for closure. A nation of watchers, children again roaming night streets, grown men clutching coffee, mothers whispering relief—each must decide how much was justice, how much was wrath masked as duty. In the bruises on Frein's face, some see only the price of capture; others, the shadow of revenge: where law bends, ever so slightly, to the ache of old grief.

When the end finally arrived, 48 days later, in the hollowed-out shell of an abandoned airport hangar, the inventory of Eric Frein's life was laid bare. He was taken without the blaze of glory he had perhaps envisioned. On his person was a collection of items that spoke to the strange, disjointed reality he inhabited: a bottle of Korean vodka to dull the cold, a laptop computer used to poach Wi-Fi signals from the civilized world he claimed to reject, 200 rounds of ammunition for a war that never came, and two pipe bombs. It was a survivalist's cache, a bizarre mixture of the lethal and the mundane, found in the possession of a man who had tried to stop time, only to find that time, inevitably, had cornered him.

There exists, among those who wear the badge, a fellowship as taut and specialized as a hangman's knot. It is a bond frequently misconstrued by the civilian mind, often dismissed with the cynical shorthand of the "Blue Wall of Silence"—a phrase that suggests a mere conspiracy of shadows. Yet, the reality is a far more intricate architecture of the spirit. It is a brotherhood forged in the shared anticipation of the worst thing that can happen.

When the news broke of the shootings at the Blooming Grove barracks, the response was a tidal wave that defied the usual mechanics of a fugitive hunt. The deployment of men, women, and the cold steel machinery of the State was practically unparalleled in the history of the Commonwealth. This was no ordinary pursuit; it was a mobilization of grief. One might ask what fuel drives such a gargantuan engine. In the grim ledger of law enforcement, there resides an unshakeable dogma: if the protectors themselves cannot be protected, then the very concept of order is a ghost, a thin vapor in the wind.

But beneath the tactical vests and the bristling rifles of the FBI and the Customs and Border Patrol, a deeper, more corrosive sentiment took root. Sergeant Damon Bee, Ret., a man who had spent his years as a patrol officer, a SWAT specialist, and a K9 handler in the quiet corners of Warren County, New Jersey, understood the anatomy of this feeling. He knew that when an officer is cut down, the wound bleeds across the entire profession. It is not merely a hunger for retribution that drives them into the damp, dark woods; it is not the simple desire for the finality of a closed case.

Instead, as Bee observed, it is the cold, crystalline realization that the fallen man is a mirror. It is the sudden, shivering awareness that the officer lying in the mountain dirt could have been you—that his blood and your blood share the same frequency. Every bullet fired at a uniform is a bullet fired at the collective heart of the service. It injects a sense of vulnerability that no amount of Kevlar can shield, a creeping inevitability that haunts the quiet moments of a midnight shift. It is a weight, heavy and invisible, that bows the shoulders of even the most hardened veterans.

They enter the fray with the bright, polished hope of the uninitiated, believing they can hold back the tide. But the woods are dark, and the man they hunt is a reminder of how thin the line truly is. As Sergeant Bee so somberly put it, "You go into law enforcement to change the world, but the world changes you."

THE CAPTURE

Dusk falls on the abandoned Birchwood-Pocono Airpark, a decaying monument to leisure now serving as the stage for the manhunt's quiet denouement. It is October 30.

The 48 days of terror do not end with a shootout, but with a surrender in the creeping shadows.

U.S. Marshals Scott Malkowski and John Schaaf, members of the elite Special Operations Group, are the ones to spot him. He is a solitary figure walking toward the hollowed-out hangar, a man returning to his lair. Malkowski moves first, securing the fugitive, while Schaaf steps in to apply the steel cuffs. The chaos of the search condenses into this singular, hushed moment.

The prisoner is calm. When asked for his name, he offers it without hesitation: "Eric Frein."

When asked for weapons, he reveals the smallness of his immediate threat: "No, I have a pocket knife."

But then, a moment of bizarre solicitude. The man who has spent weeks as a phantom in the woods, the architect of an ambush, suddenly displays a fastidious concern for public safety. He looks at Schaaf and volunteers the geography of his arsenal. "Can I tell you where the guns are located inside the hangar?" he asks.

He draws a verbal map, precise and helpful. "I have two rifles. They're on the upstairs of the hangar. You'll have to go up some stairs and walk to the end and you'll find the rifles there."

He pauses, then adds a detail that borders on the surreal. "There's a loaded pistol that's on the bottom floor and the pistol is loaded and I want to tell you this to make sure that you guys find it because I don't want a kid to find the gun."

Inside the hangar, the reality aligns perfectly with the confession.

Sergeant Michael Joyce's diagram becomes the floorplan of the fugitive's life. The two rifles are exactly where promised, resting in the gloom of the upper level. The pistol waits below. But beyond the firearms, the hangar holds a darker collection—a chemistry set of intent.

The FBI's analysis uncovers the true nature of Frein's preparations. It is a collection of "low explosives"—black powder and Pyrodex—substances that, while stable on their own, become engines of death when tightly confined.

There is lead styphnate, a chemical compound of extreme sensitivity, volatile enough to wake at the slightest shock or friction. There are the innocent components of celebration— party poppers—stripped of their joy and harvested for their red phosphorus and potassium chlorate, the friction materials needed to spark a catastrophe.

The devices themselves are crude, ugly things.

One is fully assembled, a pipe bomb packed with black powder and a hobby fuse. But it is the casing that reveals the malice: 51 metal nuts are taped to the exterior. A second device, partially finished, waits with 74 nuts. These are not designed for demolition; they are designed for flesh. They are fragmentation grenades, engineered to turn a mechanical explosion into a cloud of shrapnel.

And there is the wire.

A green-coated wire, simple and domestic, winds through the evidence. It matches the wire found on the trip mechanisms—victim-actuated switches designed to be triggered by an unsuspecting footfall. It is a metallurgical match, an iron core wrapped in a specific recipe of barium, zinc, and lead.

On the black electrical tape that binds these machines of death, the final seal of ownership is found.

The latent prints do not lie. They are lifted from the adhesive and the smooth surfaces of the pipe bombs, three distinct impressions that belong to only one man. They act as a signature on the work, confirming that the hands that surrendered in the dusk are the same hands that carefully, methodically, wrapped the tape around the steel, preparing for a war that ended with a whisper.

IN THE GRASP

On October 30, 2014, the sun began to dip below the ridge of the Pocono Mountains, casting long, skeletal shadows across the decaying tarmac of the Birchwood-Pocono Airpark. It was a place where the American dream of leisure had gone to rot—a honeymoon resort once teeming with lovers and private planes, now reduced to a hollowed-out ghost town of broken glass and rusted hangars. The silence here was not peaceful; it was the heavy, expectant silence of a stage waiting for its final act.

Into this graveyard of 1960s optimism stepped the U.S. Marshals.

They moved with the quiet, lethal efficiency of men who hunt other men for a living. Deputy Marshal Scott Malkowski and his team from the Special Operations Group swept through the tall grass, their boots crushing the weeds that had reclaimed the runway. They were not looking for romance; they were looking for a phantom. For 48 days, Eric Matthew Frein had been a ghost, a rumor in the woods, a shape that dissolved into the treeline just as the thermal cameras swept past. He had humiliated the state police, terrified a community, and turned the Pennsylvania wilderness into his private theater of war.

But every performance must end.

Malkowski saw him first. He was not the Rambo-esque figure of the public's terrified imagination, nor the Serbian soldier of his own delusions. He was a solitary, wretched figure walking across the open field near the hangar, exposed and careless. He looked small against the backdrop of the towering pines, a man diminished by weeks of cold rain and a diet of tuna fish. The marshal did not shout; he did not fire. He simply closed the distance, the way a wolf closes on a wounded deer, and the gap between the hunter and the hunted vanished.

"Police!"

The command shattered the stillness. Frein did not run. He did not reach for the rifle that had ended one life and ruined another. He simply froze, his hands rising in a gesture of absolute surrender, the fight draining out of him like water from a cracked vessel. He went down to his knees, then to his belly, pressing his face into the cold, unforgiving earth. When they cuffed him, the metal clicking shut with a finality that echoed across the empty airfield, they found he was unarmed but for a pocket knife.

He looked up at them, his face gaunt and scraped, a cut on his nose bleeding sluggishly.

"Can I tell you where the guns are located inside the hangar?" he asked, his voice polite, almost helpful, as if he were a tour guide pointing out local landmarks rather than a domestic terrorist confessing to his arsenal. He described the location of the rifles upstairs and the loaded pistol below with a fastidious precision, anxious that no child should find them. It was a bizarre moment of domestic solicitude from a man who had spent seven weeks holding an entire region hostage with the threat of indiscriminate death.

Inside the hangar, the inventory of his life was laid bare.

It was a pathetic collection, a survivalist's cache that spoke more of loneliness than revolution. There were the tools of his violence, yes—the rifles, the ammunition—but there were also the artifacts of his solitude: a bottle of Korean vodka, a laptop, and DVDs to pass the long, empty hours. He had sought to be a warrior, a political assassin who would wake the nation from its slumber. Instead, he was found shivering in a ruin, a man who had traded his humanity for a few weeks of notoriety and a pair of stolen handcuffs— Corporal Dickson's handcuffs—which now bound his wrists as he was led away, not to glory, but to a cage.

WORDS IN THE FLUORESCENT DARK

It was not a bound volume, this testament to a private war, but a sodden collection of debris retrieved from the refuse of a campsite. The pages were water-logged, staining the hands of the men who found them, tucked away in a trash bag like the discarded wrappers of a finished meal. Alongside these damp, handwritten sheets lay a thumb drive, a digital capsule containing the final, polished thoughts of a man who believed he was writing for history.

Together, these fragments formed the autobiography of a phantom.

The handwritten entries, scrawled in the aftermath of the violence, possessed a chilling, clinical dryness. There was no rage in the ink, no tremors of conscience, only the flat, observational tone of a pathologist noting the time of death. Of that Friday, September 12, he wrote: "Got a shot around 11 p.m. and took it."

The detachment was absolute. "He dropped. I was surprised at how quick."

It was a study in physics, not murder. He recorded the "follow-up shot" to the head and neck not as a brutality, but as a procedure, noting with satisfaction that the target was "still and quiet after that." When a second trooper appeared, attempting to aid the fallen, the sniper's eye remained unblinking. "As he went to kneel, I took a shot at him and [he] jumped in the door. His legs were visible and still." Upon reading these lines, the police would call it pure evil; the author, however, seemed to view it merely as a successful day's work.

But the god-like distance of the sniper's perch did not last. The narrative shifted rapidly from the omnipotent to the desperate. The grand exit strategy, the motorized flight into the night, ended in the muddy water of a retention pond near the barracks. The Jeep, his vessel of escape, had failed him. "Jeep ran into a swamp," he scribbled, the frustration palpable. "Disaster."

He was forced to shed the heavy machinery of his war. "Made it out with rifle and pack... had to dump the AK." The woods, dark and indifferent, swallowed him.

On the thumb drive, however, the tone was different. Here, in a letter addressed to his parents, he attempted to drape his violence in the heavy robes of patriotism. He spoke of a nation "far from what it was," a country in decay that he, a solitary executioner, sought to redeem. "There is so much wrong and on so many levels," he typed, "only passing through the crucible of another revolution can get us back the liberties we once had."

He fancied himself a catalyst, a historical inevitability. "Tension is high at the moment and the time seems right for a spark to ignite a fire in the hearts of men." He acknowledged the novelty of his crime, admitting, "What I have done has not been done before and it felt like it was worth a try."

Yet, beneath the revolutionary rhetoric, the small, disappointed voice of a son broke through. The grandiose political assassin dissolved into a man apologizing for a wasted life. "I am sorry," he wrote to the mother and father he would never see as a free man again. "You guys are great parents, I am just not a good son." He confessed to squandering opportunity, to a life of mediocrity that culminated in this final, terrible gesture.

What followed in the handwritten notes was the logbook of a creature hunted. He treated the manhunt not as a pursuit, but as a war game, a strategic exercise played out in the dirt and the laurel. He became a student of his pursuers, memorizing the flight patterns of the helicopters, learning the rhythm of their refueling, listening to the static of the police scanners like a lullaby.

He existed in the thin, terrifying margins of the search. At times, the hunters were close enough to touch. He noted with a terrifying intimacy that the lawmen were "about a football field away," blind to the eyes watching them from the brush. He moved through the emptiness of the vacation cabins, scavenging for food, a ghost haunting the locked rooms of the unaware, waiting for the inevitable end of the game.

The confession room at the Blooming Grove barracks possessed all the sterile anonymity of a doctor's examination room: white walls, harsh fluorescent lighting, the kind of institutional furniture that seemed designed to strip away pretense and reveal the essential truth beneath. It was here, on the night of October 30, 2014, that Eric Matthew Frein would deliver his final performance, though he perhaps did not yet understand that the role he had inhabited for 48 days was finally coming to an end.

The videotaped interview that jurors would later watch unfold over three hours revealed something both startling and utterly predictable. Here was a man who appeared almost disappointingly ordinary in the harsh light of capture, no longer the phantom of the Pocono woods, no longer the Serbian soldier of his elaborate fantasies, but simply a 31-year-old man sitting across from investigators, the weight of his actions settling around him like fog.

The words, when they came, possessed a terrible simplicity that cut through months of speculation about motive and madness. "I did this. No one else did," he told his questioners, the phrase carrying the full weight of ownership, no shared responsibility, no mitigation through mental illness or political philosophy. It was, perhaps, the most honest statement he had made in years, stripping away the elaborate mythology he had constructed around himself to reveal the essential truth: a man alone with his grievances and his rifle.

Yet even in confession, Frein could not entirely abandon the grandiose narrative that had sustained him through his weeks in the wilderness. The investigators would later testify that he described Corporal Bryon Dickson's death not as murder, but as an "assassination"—a word choice that elevated his act from personal violence to political statement, that transformed a husband and father into a symbol in some revolutionary drama that existed primarily in Frein's imagination.

The confession revealed a man caught between personas, struggling to reconcile the revolutionary hero of his fantasies with the increasingly unavoidable reality of what he had actually done. At moments, glimpses of genuine remorse seemed to break through the ideological armor he had constructed around himself. "All I can say is I'm sorry," he told the investigators, words that carried an almost childlike directness in their simplicity.

Sorry for what, exactly? For the death of Corporal Dickson? For the wounding of Trooper Alex Douglass? For the 48 days of terror he had inflicted upon an entire region? Or simply sorry that his grand gesture had failed to produce the awakening he had envisioned, that instead of sparking revolution, he had merely created grief and manhunts?

The video captured something else as well: the peculiar deflation that occurs when fantasy finally collides with consequence. Here was Eric Frein without his Serbian cigarettes, without his carefully curated military surplus, without the vast stage of the Pennsylvania wilderness. Just a man in a chair, answering questions about actions that had transformed him from weekend warrior into genuine monster.

The investigators, trained in the patient art of confession, allowed the silence to stretch between questions, understanding that in the fluorescent glare of that small room, truth had a way of surfacing despite all attempts to suppress it. They watched as the elaborate mythology Frein had constructed around himself—the political revolutionary, the freedom fighter, the necessary catalyst for change— slowly dissolved under the weight of simple, direct questions about what he had done and why.

What emerged was not the portrait of a political warrior that Frein had perhaps hoped to present, but something far more mundane and infinitely more tragic: a man who had convinced himself that his personal resentments constituted political philosophy, who had elevated individual grievance into historical necessity, who had mistaken the theater of violence for actual revolution.

The confession concluded not with defiant proclamations or revolutionary rhetoric, but with the quiet acknowledgment of a man who had discovered that reality, unlike his elaborate war games, offers no opportunity for reset, no chance to begin again when the outcome proves unsatisfactory. He had gotten his war and found it to be exactly what war always is: not glorious, not transformative, but simply wasteful and irreversibly, tragically real.

THE TRIAL

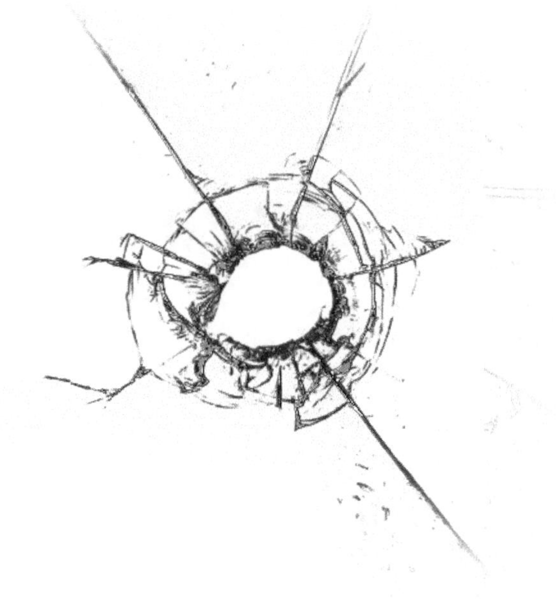

DAYS OF RECKONING

The trial that would determine Eric Frein's fate began on April 4, 2017, in the Pike County Courthouse in Milford, Pennsylvania, a stately Victorian structure that had presided over the legal affairs of this rural county since 1874. The Honorable Gregory H. Chelak, a veteran jurist with more than two decades on the bench, would oversee what promised to be one of the most closely watched capital murder cases in Pennsylvania history.

In the peculiar theater of American justice, where the fate of one man can hinge on the quality of fluorescent lighting in a courthouse corridor or the ability of 12 strangers to look beyond the surface of what they think they know about murder, the Pike County Courthouse offered its own somber grandeur. Built in the ornate style that marked public architecture in the final decades of the 19th century, the building stood as a monument to an era when communities invested their civic pride in structures that would endure for generations. Its red brick facade, weathered by more than a century of Pennsylvania winters, rose four stories above Milford's main street, crowned by a clock tower whose chimes had marked the hours for countless trials, verdicts, and the quiet passage of rural justice.

The courtroom itself, officially Courtroom Number One, bore the accumulated patina of decades spent witnessing the full spectrum of human folly and tragedy. Mahogany paneling, darkened by years of cigarette smoke from the days when such things were permitted, covered the lower half of the walls, while tall windows filtered the harsh April sunlight through panes of glass that had witnessed the legal proceedings of four generations. The ceiling, pressed tin painted in institutional beige, stretched high above the chamber, its ornate molding a reminder of the aspirations of the craftsmen who had built this temple to justice with their own hands.

During the trial of Eric Matthew Frein, the courtroom in Milford was a stage built of cold, judicial stone, yet infused with the lingering, terrible smoke of a September midnight. The entire proceeding, from the whispered legal maneuvers to the clinical recitation of violence, was the long, slow shadow of a single, malevolent act.

The day began not in the public glare, but in the close, quiet sanctum of Judge Gregory H. Chelak's chambers, where the lawyers met in a prelude to the true reckoning. The defense, led by the weary-eyed Attorney William Ruzzo, attempted a doomed maneuver, presenting a motion to appeal the suppression order—a final, fatalistic gesture to slow the inevitable momentum. Ruzzo simply "murmured that the petition spoke for itself," as if all vital arguments had been drained. District Attorney Raymond Tonkin immediately objected, asserting that such an action would be "extraordinary," a needless delay when the true justice was at hand. The judge's pen delivered the final verdict: the motion was denied. A small, necessary skirmish was lost.

In the tight-knit geography of Pike County, the line between the prosecutor's office and the barracks is non-existent. For Ray Tonkin, this was not abstract case law. He had stood at crime scenes with these men; he had taken their calls in the middle of the night; he had trusted them with the safety of the community he was sworn to protect. The death of Corporal Dickson was not a file on a desk—it was an empty seat at a table he knew well.

When the time came to sign the notice of aggravating circumstances—the formal declaration that the Commonwealth would seek Eric Frein's life—his hand did not shake. To Tonkin, the death penalty was not a political stance but a moral necessity, the only currency valuable enough to pay for the theft of a protector. He carried into the courtroom not just the statutes of Pennsylvania, but the collective, simmering rage of a fraternity that had been hunted in the dark.

The prosecutor who would seek justice for the fallen trooper was District Attorney Ray Tonkin, a man whose voice carried the weight of the Commonwealth. His career embodied the kind of steady progression through Pennsylvania's legal system that marked the most effective public servants. At 54 years old, Tonkin cut an impressive figure in the courtroom—a tall, broad-shouldered man whose commanding presence reflected his background as both an athlete and a prosecutor. His prematurely gray hair and sharp blue eyes conveyed the kind of prosecutorial intensity that had made him one of Pennsylvania's most respected district attorneys, while his deep, resonant voice carried easily to the back of any courtroom.

Tonkin had graduated with honors from the University of Pittsburgh School of Law after earning his undergraduate degree in criminal justice from the University of Scranton— credentials that reflected both intellectual capability and a dedication to law enforcement that would define his professional life.

Tonkin's rise to the district attorney's office had followed the traditional path of ambitious prosecutors. He had joined the Pike County District Attorney's Office in 1999 as an assistant district attorney, spending eight years learning the craft of criminal prosecution under the mentorship of seasoned attorneys who had handled every variety of case that rural Pennsylvania could produce. His elevation to district attorney 11 years before the Frein case had given him extensive experience with capital murder prosecutions, but none had carried the personal stakes and public scrutiny that would define this particular trial.

Tonkin understood the theater of the courtroom better than anyone in Milford, and he had anticipated the defense's script long before opening statements. He knew they would try to paint Frein as a "broken boy," a victim of a domineering father and a fragile psyche. Tonkin's strategy was to be the cold wall of reality against which that narrative would shatter. He would not be flamboyant; he would be relentless. He intended to pile the forensic facts—the casings, the diary, the bombs—brick by brick until the image of the "lost child" was buried beneath the weight of his own calculated malice. He treated the trial not as a debate but as a siege, and he intended to give no quarter.

For both men, the Frein case represented the culmination of legal careers spent preparing for exactly this kind of challenge—a capital murder case with national implications, involving the assassination of a law enforcement officer by a domestic terrorist whose actions had paralyzed an entire region. The weight of that responsibility was evident in every procedural decision, every ruling from the bench, every strategic choice made by the prosecution.

On that first morning of trial, as court personnel made their final preparations and the bailiff called the session to order, there was in the air that peculiar tension that attends only the most serious criminal proceedings—the knowledge that over the coming days, 12 ordinary citizens would be asked to weigh evidence and render judgment on whether the State should take the life of one of its own citizens.

Eric Frein, seated quietly behind the counsel table, denied every accusation that faced him. The indictment was as heavy as the still air in the Pike County courtroom, 12 counts exposed like a prosecutor's ledger of violence and intent.

Murder in the first degree—a cold and deliberate strike at the heart of law and order. An attempt to commit that same act, a shadow of destruction hanging just as heavily.

Among these formal pronouncements were charges that carried a particular weight, marking not only a man but an assault upon the very symbols of the State. The first-degree murder of a law enforcement officer, a crime that transfers grief from the singular to the collective, was followed closely by attempted murder of that same ilk. Assault, raw and physical, punctuated the list like bursts of gunfire.

Two counts of terrorism—terms that confound law and morality—with Frein accused of seeking to terrorize not a single soul, but the state itself, its citizens writ small beneath his calculated shadow. Coupled with these were two charges of wielding weapons of mass destruction, the crude terror of pipe bombs and the sinister certainty of explosive intent.

His indictment further cataloged the discharge of a firearm into an occupied structure, a reckless act of terror, and the possession of instruments tailored to crime, all bound by the law's firm hand under recklessly endangering another. It was a litany born of a calculated rampage—the fatal bullet that stole Corporal Bryon K. Dickson II's life, the wounded body of Trooper Alex Douglass, and the strung intervals of fear punctuating a 48-day manhunt, a shadow-play of violence and menace etched into Pennsylvania's wooded ridge.

The charges were not mere words; they were the echoes of a man's defiance against a community's peace, the legal summoning of justice to a place still haunted by a single night's dark betrayal.

The defendant himself sat at the counsel table with the kind of studied composure that comes either from genuine indifference or the most carefully constructed psychological armor. Eric Matthew Frein, now 33 years old and bearing the pallor that marks men who have spent months in the artificial lighting of maximum security facilities, presented a figure both ordinary and unsettling. Gone was the modified Mohawk haircut that had marked his transformation from suburban malcontent to domestic terrorist; in its place was the regulation short cut mandated by Pennsylvania's correctional system. His dark eyes, set in a face that had grown gaunt during his incarceration, moved methodically around the courtroom, taking in the gallery filled with law enforcement officers, the jury box that would soon hold his judges, the witness stand where the consequences of his actions would be laid bare in clinical detail.

There was about Frein a curious quality of detachment, as if he were observing these proceedings from some great distance rather than sitting at their center. He wore the standard-issue civilian clothes provided for defendants in capital cases—a navy blue suit that hung loose on his diminished frame, a white shirt that emphasized the pallor of his complexion, a conservative tie that transformed him into something resembling an accountant or insurance salesman rather than a man who had ambushed police officers from the Pennsylvania woodland. It was a costume, really, designed to present to the jury the most unthreatening version of a man whose actions had terrorized two counties and left one family permanently shattered.

His defense attorneys, Michael Weinstein and William Ruzzo, both seasoned practitioners of criminal law who had drawn the unenviable task of defending the indefensible, flanked him at the counsel table like bookends supporting a volume that no one particularly wanted to read. Weinstein, a tall, angular man with graying hair and the kind of intense brown eyes that missed nothing, had built his reputation defending capital cases throughout eastern Pennsylvania. His partner, Ruzzo, was shorter and more compact, with the kind of nervous energy that manifested in constant note-taking and frequent whispered conferences with his client.

The impossible client sat across from Michael Weinstein in the attorney-client conference room at Pike County Correctional Facility, his expression as bland as milk, discussing his own death with the detachment of a man reviewing a restaurant menu. This was the particular hell of capital defense work: not merely that your client was guilty—they were almost always guilty—but that they often possessed no vocabulary for remorse, no grammar for acknowledging the enormity of what they had done.

Michael Weinstein had been defending capital cases for nearly three decades. He had developed, over those years, a kind of professional callus against the emotional demands of the work. You represented the system, he told himself, not the man. You ensured that even the most despised defendant received the vigorous advocacy that the Constitution demanded. But Eric Matthew Frein tested even this carefully constructed philosophy.

The evidence was suffocating in its completeness. The videotaped confession alone would have been sufficient for conviction—three hours of Frein calmly describing his preparations, his execution of the ambush, his weeks of evasion. But the prosecution had layered onto this foundation a mountain of physical evidence: DNA, ballistics, computer searches, handwritten journals, pipe bombs. It was not a case to be won, merely a disaster to be managed.

Weinstein had suggested, early on, that they pursue an insanity defense. Surely a man who had spent years preparing to murder police officers, who kept journals documenting his anti-government ideology, who transformed himself into a Serbian soldier for weekend war games could not be considered sane by any reasonable definition.

But Frein had refused. "I knew what I was doing," he had said, his voice carrying that maddening flatness. "I'm not crazy."

Both men understood the almost impossible nature of their task: how does one defend a man whose guilt is established by video confession, physical evidence, and the testimony of his surviving victim?

On the night of October 30, 2014, in a sterile interview room at the Blooming Grove barracks—the very place where his deadly theater had begun 48 days earlier—Eric Matthew Frein had given what would prove to be his final performance. The manhunt was over, the woods had surrendered their secret, and the man who had transformed himself into a phantom was suddenly, irrevocably present again.

The videotaped confession that jurors would later watch unfold across three hours revealed something both more and less than they had expected. Here was no wild-eyed fanatic ranting about revolution, no theatrical villain delivering grandiose soliloquies about his cause. Instead, they witnessed a man who appeared, in the fluorescent glare of the interrogation room, almost disappointingly ordinary. Frein was comfortable—sipping coffee and smoking cigars, as if he were settling in for a casual evening conversation rather than confessing to acts that had terrorized an entire region.

The words, when they came, possessed a chilling simplicity. "I did this. No one else did," he told his questioners, the phrase carrying the weight of absolute ownership—no shared blame, no mitigation through conspiracy or coercion. It was, perhaps, the most honest thing he had said in years, stripping away the layers of Serbian soldier personas and revolutionary fantasies to reveal the essential truth: a man alone with his grievances and his rifle.

Yet even in confession, Frein could not entirely abandon his role as political actor. Police have said Frein acknowledged Dickson's slaying was an "assassination" and that he did it to change government and "wake people up." The choice of the word "assassination" was telling—not "murder," not "killing," but a term that elevated his act from personal violence to political statement, that transformed Corporal Bryon Dickson II from a man with a wife and children into a symbol in some larger drama that existed primarily in Frein's imagination.

This grandiose delusion extended beyond the immediate confession. In a letter Frein wrote to his parents, he said that only "another revolution can get us back to the liberties we once had," revealing how completely he had convinced himself that his ambush was not an act of terrorism but the opening shot of some necessary uprising. The letter provided a window into a mind that had transformed personal resentment into political philosophy, that had elevated individual grievance into historical necessity.

Perhaps most remarkably, even as he accepted responsibility for his actions, Frein offered what seemed like genuine remorse in his confession to his captors. The video revealed a man caught between personas: part political revolutionary, part remorseful criminal, part weary performer finally stepping out of character. The three hours of questioning stripped away, layer by layer, the mythology he had constructed around himself. The Serbian cigarettes, the military surplus uniforms, the elaborate survival caches— all were reduced to evidence in a criminal case rather than props in his grand performance.

In the end, the confession video served as a kind of autopsy of a delusion. Here was Eric Frein without his costume, without his stage, without his audience of terrified communities and pursuing law enforcement. The confession concluded not with revolutionary rhetoric or defiant proclamations, but with the quiet acknowledgment of a man who had discovered that reality, unlike his reenactments, offers no opportunity for do-overs, no chance to reset the game when the outcome proves unsatisfactory.

INSTRUMENTS OF JUSTICE

The selection of the jury had proven extraordinarily difficult, requiring the Court to summon potential jurors from Chester County because of the extensive publicity the case had generated in the Poconos. Chester County is 148 miles from the courthouse, a 2-hour-and-40-minute-long drive. It took them from Interstate-76 West, 476 North, Interstate-81 North, Interstate-84 East and, finally, US-6 East. It was quite a trudge.

The process took weeks, as attorneys searched for 12 citizens who could render an impartial verdict despite the saturation coverage that had made Eric Frein's name synonymous with cop killing throughout eastern Pennsylvania.

The jury that finally emerged from this painstaking process represented a cross-section of Pennsylvania society—men and women from diverse backgrounds who had been selected not just for their ability to be fair, but for their willingness to endure what everyone knew would be an emotionally grueling ordeal. It consisted of farmers and factory workers, retirees and middle managers, housewives and small business owners. They ranged in age from their early 20s to their late 60s, their faces bearing the kind of earnest attention that citizens bring to the most serious responsibilities of democratic participation.

Among them was Margaret Kowalski, a 62-year-old retired school teacher from Chester County whose gray hair and wire-rimmed glasses gave her the appearance of someone accustomed to maintaining order in chaotic situations. Her hands, folded carefully in her lap, bore the calluses of decades spent tending to the small farm she shared with her husband, while her blue eyes held the kind of patient wisdom that comes from years spent guiding young people through the complexities of growing up.

Margaret Kowalski had taught sixth-grade social studies for 37 years, a career that had equipped her with certain useful skills: the ability to maintain order in chaos, to parse competing narratives, to recognize when someone was lying. She had retired two years before receiving her jury summons and had imagined that her days of adjudicating disputes were behind her. The universe, apparently, had other plans.

The jury room at the Pike County Courthouse was smaller than her old classroom and considerably less cheerful. Gray walls, a table scarred by decades of deliberation, chairs that squeaked when you shifted your weight. It smelled faintly of industrial cleaner and old coffee. Here, she and 11 strangers would determine whether a man would live or die.

She had not wanted to be foreman. The position had been thrust upon her during the initial deliberations through a process that seemed to involve her being the oldest person present and the only one willing to make eye contact when the question was raised. Now she sat at the head of the table, a yellow legal pad before her, and felt the weight of responsibility settling onto her shoulders like a heavy coat.

Beside her sat James Morrison, 45 years old and employed as a shift supervisor at a paper mill in Chester County. His broad shoulders and work-roughened hands spoke to a life spent in physical labor, while his steady brown eyes reflected the kind of common sense that working-class Americans bring to their civic duties. He wore his best suit—navy blue and carefully pressed—and a tie that his wife had selected for the occasion, understanding instinctively that serving on a jury in a capital murder case required one's finest attire.

In the front row of the jury box, Sarah Chen, 28 years old and employed as an accountant at a regional firm, represented the younger generation of Americans called to this solemn duty. Her black hair was pulled back in a professional style, while her dark eyes held the kind of analytical intelligence that her profession required. She took notes constantly, her pen moving across a small notebook with the precision that marked her approach to all of life's complexities.

These three citizens, along with nine others selected from hundreds of potential jurors and sworn to render impartial judgment, would spend the next three weeks listening to testimony that would test their ability to remain objective in the face of evidence that was both overwhelming in its completeness and devastating in its implications. They would be asked to look beyond their natural revulsion at Frein's actions and determine not just his guilt—which seemed hardly in question—but whether his crimes warranted the ultimate penalty that the Commonwealth of Pennsylvania could impose.

The jurors themselves became part of the courtroom drama, though their identities remained protected by the Court. They were required to stay in the Milford area Monday through Friday for what could be up to seven weeks of testimony, a significant personal hardship that spoke to the gravity of the case. As one court official noted, "It's clearly

going to be a hardship and they'll have to adjust to it"—
an understatement that barely captured the toll such service
would take on ordinary citizens thrust into the center of a
capital murder trial.

In the sterile, fluorescent-lit theater of the Pike County
Courthouse, a most peculiar fellowship was forged—a
fraternity of 12 ordinary souls, uprooted from the familiar
comforts of Chester County and transplanted, like specimen
plants, into the rugged, unsettling soil of Milford. This was a
"change of venire," a legal maneuver meant to ensure a fair
trial, but for the jurors—retirees like Margaret Kowalski and
shift supervisors like James Morrison—it was a sentence of
seven weeks in a land of motels and shared silences.

Every Monday, they made the 148-mile pilgrimage across
the Commonwealth, leaving behind their farms and
accounting firms to inhabit a repetitive cycle of hotel rooms
and courthouse corridors. It was a "significant personal
hardship," a term that barely captured the surreal logistics
of their isolation. They lived out of suitcases, their identities
momentarily reduced to a number and a seat in a pre-
assigned row.

Their fraternity was one of forced social performance. Bound
by a strict decorum that forbade them from discussing the
very thing that bound them together, they shared countless
meals and morning coffees in a hollow kind of bonding,
avoiding the case like a specter at the dinner table. They
became experts in the mundane, discussing the weather or
the quality of the hotel breakfast, while their minds remained
heavy with the graphic evidence of the day.

The psychological weight was immense. They were far
from home, yet trapped in the "Frein Zone," forced to
stare into the catastrophic trauma of autopsy photographs
and the muttered words of the dying. They sat in the jury

box, witnesses to a three-hour confession where a cigar-smoking Eric Frein casually recounted an "assassination," and they watched Trooper Alex Douglass walk to the stand on a prosthetic leg—a permanent, physical reminder of one September midnight.

The isolation reached its peak in the deliberation room—a windowless chamber that smelled of industrial cleaner and old coffee. Here, Margaret Kowalski led 11 strangers through the "most difficult thing" they would ever do. When the verdict was finally rendered, the judge dismissed them back to the "privacy of your own lives," ordering the destruction of their notes and the sealing of their thoughts. They returned across those 148 miles, not with satisfaction, but with an "immense weariness," carrying the burden of a home that no longer felt quite so safe.

The 12 citizens who filed into the jury box each morning were not of the Poconos. They had been imported, like rare goods, from Chester County—a landscape of manicured lawns, equestrian estates, and the soft, affluent hum of the Philadelphia Main Line. They were strangers in a strange land, tasked with judging a crime born of the mountains.

The distance was measured in more than miles. It was a cultural chasm. In Pike County, the woods are a place of utility and harvest; a man walking with a rifle is as common as a mailbox. The "survivalist" impulse, the stocking of the larder, the knowledge of the deer trail—these are not aberrations; they are heritage.

But to the jurors from the suburbs, where the woods are a backdrop for jogging and the only weapon is a security system, Eric Frein must have appeared as a creature from a different century. The defense's attempt to paint him as a "woodsman," a skilled reenactor merely playing a part that went wrong, may have backfired in the most catastrophic way. To a suburban jury, the very idea of a "militia," of spending weekends in the dirt pretending to be a Serbian soldier, likely read not as a hobby, but as a pathology.

They did not see a "local boy gone wrong." They saw a monster who had emerged from a wilderness they did not understand. The hunting culture of the Poconos, rather than humanizing Frein, may have served to make him even more alien, more dangerous. In their eyes, he was not just a killer; he was the embodiment of a rural darkness, a savage reminder of what lay beyond the safety of their streetlights. The change of venire, intended to ensure fairness, may instead have ensured his doom, placing his fate in the hands of people who viewed his entire world with a deep, instinctive suspicion.

THE HATED MEN

In the hierarchy of pariahs, the only person lower than the child killer is the man who stands next to him and says, "Not so fast."

Michael Weinstein and William Ruzzo understood this. They were the Defense, the "Devil's Advocates," tasked with the constitutional duty of saving a man whom the entire county wished to see dead. To walk into a diner in Milford was to feel the temperature drop. The stares were not curious; they were hostile. The waitresses served the coffee with a clatter of silverware that felt like an accusation. *How can you?* the eyes asked. *How can you sit there and defend him?*

They received the hate mail, the anonymous threats, the late-night calls. It is a psychological burden that few can understand—the weight of knowing that your best work will result in the survival of a monster, and your failure will result in a State-sponsored execution.

Their meetings with Frein were studies in frustration. They would go to the Pike County Correctional Facility, passing through the layers of security to the sterile, windowless conference room. They needed a client who would give them something to work with—remorse, tears, madness, anything.

Instead, they got Eric.

He was polite. He was calm. He was maddeningly detached. He spoke of the ambush as if it were a tactical exercise that had gone well and his capture as a logistical error. He showed no emotion for the widow weeping in the front row, no flicker of recognition for the devastation he had caused. He was a hollow man, a void where a conscience should have been.

Desperate, the defense turned to the mitigation specialists, the archeologists of trauma. They sent investigators to the childhood home, to the schools, to the neighbors, digging for the "why." They were looking for the abuse, the head injury, the defining trauma that could explain the inexplicable. They needed a narrative of brokenness to counter the prosecution's narrative of evil. But what they found was more disturbing: a slow, quiet slide into darkness, greased by the lies of a father and the isolation of a son, a banality that defied the magnitude of the crime.

William Ruzzo and Michael Weinstein carried the burden of the pariah. Late at night, in offices dim with the smoke of exhaustion, they sifted through the wreckage of Eric Frein's life, searching for a shard of humanity amid the debris of his delusions. They needed a tragedy to counter the horror; they found only the banality of a quiet, broken boy and a father's stolen valor.

They sat across from their client in the sterile, windowless conference room, searching his flat, empty eyes for a flicker of remorse, a tremor of fear, anything that might prove he was still tethered to the human race. But Frein gave them nothing but the polite detachment of a tourist discussing a trip gone wrong, leaving his defenders to drink their whiskey alone in the dark, wondering if they were fighting for a man or merely for the abstract, indifferent principle of the law.

FORENSIC TRAIL

Master Trooper Sean Doran of the Forensic Services Unit, a veteran of nearly 25 years, was called to the scene around 2:00 a.m. on September 13. His duties, shared with Trooper Hitchcock, were to process the scene: documenting, photographing, and collecting evidence.

Upon ascending to the main floor, Doran observed the body of Corporal Dickson in the hallway, covered with a yellow emergency blanket. He photographed the scene extensively, including the bullet hole in the chest area of Dickson's ballistic vest carrier, which was "very minute" in the front but "considerably larger" in the rear, indicating a through-and-through shot. He confirmed that the under-uniform vests were not rated for rifle rounds.

In the lobby, Doran documented blood on the floor, a smashed pane of the glass entrance door, and damage to the Communications Room window. He recovered a projectile that had been stuck in a damaged newspaper on a shelf near the Communications Room window. He also documented a bullet fragment found on the lobby floor, a damaged duty belt, and a tactical flashlight at the base of the damaged glass door.

As the trial progressed through its various phases, the jury's behavior revealed the psychological complexity of their task. During the penalty phase, when Frein's family members testified about his troubled childhood and difficult relationship with his parents, several jurors leaned forward in their seats, clearly weighing the mitigation evidence against the overwhelming proof of his guilt. Their faces showed the internal struggle that defines capital cases—the tension between justice and mercy, between the desire for retribution and the recognition of human complexity.

The courtroom in Milford, Pennsylvania once again settled into its grim rhythm for the third day of the Commonwealth's case against Eric Matthew Frein. This installment of the trial was devoted entirely to the cold, undeniable evidence—the meticulous maps of the crime, the spent brass in the woods, and the abandoned vehicle, a green Jeep Cherokee that proved to be the killer's discarded signature. The testimonies wove together a tale of precision both in the attack and in the subsequent, methodical police response.

The morning began with Trooper Mark Pizzuti, a member of the Criminal Investigation Unit at Blooming Grove. Pizzuti, a former member of the Forensic Services Unit, described the critical search operation executed on the morning of September 13, 2014.

He explained that after initial analysis by the Forensic Unit, it was deemed "likely that the direction of fire towards the barracks was from the west, westerly side"—that is, across State Route 402. Pizzuti, organizing "several dozen law enforcement officers" into a "straight line search," described the chilling exactitude required: the search was "very slow methodical" and at a "snail's pace," with members "literally searching inch by inch."

Approximately 85 to 90 feet into the woods, the line halted when Trooper George Murphy "sounded off: 'shell casing.' " Pizzuti and Trooper Victor Quinones then joined Murphy, and within a small, imaginary three-to-four-foot circle, they located four total brass cartridge casings. These spent casings, all stamped "AFF 88," were subsequently photographed and collected.

Following Pizzuti was Sergeant Michael Joyce, a collision analysis and reconstruction specialist (CARS Unit). Joyce's testimony focused on forensic mapping, the precise art of surveying a crime scene using a Total Station—a tripod-mounted instrument akin to a surveyor's tool.

Joyce presented three crucial diagrams:

Exhibit 83, a diagram of the barracks' main floor, detailing the layout of the Communications Room, Patrol Corporal's Office, and the Patrol Room, which housed the arms locker.

Exhibit 84, a detailed evidence map marking where items were found within the barracks. This included Corporal Dickson's body, blood drops, a magazine, a vest, and a portable radio, showing the locations of three reference points used for mapping.

Exhibit 85, the overall diagram, which superimposed the key evidence onto a wide view encompassing the barracks, Route 402, and the woods. Joyce confirmed the critical distance. "It was approximately 257 feet from the spent casings to the front door of the barracks." He also mapped two "bullet strikes" in trees, located approximately 70 feet from the spent casings, to relate the evidence found to the line of fire.

THE DNA CONNECTION

Lauren Force, a Forensic Scientist II with the Pennsylvania State Police DNA Division, testified as an expert in DNA analysis. Force explained that DNA analysis involves examining short tandem repeats (STRs) at highly variable areas, looking at 16 total areas (loci) to generate a profile. As always, reality lies hidden in the grains of its composition.

The truth of a man or woman, hidden from the human eye and the witness's fallible memory, rests in a molecule of terrifying intimacy: deoxyribonucleic acid, commonly known as DNA. It is a blueprint, an instruction manual, unique to every soul save those few identical twins born into the world. And every person, every soul who moves and breathes, leaves a trail of it everywhere they go—a trace of blood, a breath of saliva, the unseen residue of skin cells left merely by the brush of a hand against a rifle stock.

For the officers of the law, this molecule is a fate written in miniature, the final, cold geometry that eliminates doubt. Yet, one must understand that the forensic scientist does not read the entire three billion base pairs of that genetic novel. That would be a labor beyond human patience. Instead, the analyst focuses on the profound and telling differences— the one-tenth of one percent of the code that separates one person from the next.

This crucial difference is found in certain areas of the genetic thread, regions of "short repeating sequences" known as short tandem repeats (STRs). Imagine a phrase—say, TATT—repeated again and again. One person may inherit a sequence repeated eight times from their mother and 12 times from their father; another may have 10 and 14. This variable number of repeats, which scientists call alleles, at specific locations, or loci, is the heart of the investigation.

In the case of a crime, the great challenge is often quantity. The sample may be "low level" or "degraded"—a mere smear, or "touch DNA" left on a cigarette butt in the mud. To conquer this silence, the scientist employs a marvelous piece of chemistry called the polymerase chain reaction (PCR). This process makes millions of copies of those tiny, telling STR segments, amplifying the whisper into a shout so that it may be heard and measured.

The resulting fragments are then sorted by size, often using a fine electrical current that pulls them through a narrow tube. They emerge as a distinct sequence of peaks on a chart—the DNA profile. This combination of peaks at the designated 13 or more loci creates the individual's genetic fingerprint.

The final act is comparison: the analyst simply lays the profile taken from the forensic unknown—the biological material found at the scene—against the reference profile of the accused. If all the alleles match, that is, if the peaks fall at the exact same left-to-right position, then a statistical calculation is performed. Given a sufficient number of these markers, the chance that two unrelated persons will share all of them becomes "vanishingly small"—a probability often measured in the quintillions, proving a connection with a cold, irrefutable certainty that no amount of human defense can challenge. It is the signature of fate itself.

Force confirmed that the known sample (K8) taken from Eric Matthew Frein was a single source profile. She then compared this to multiple items of evidence processed by Brunee Coolbaugh (PSP Serology).

Force delivered the following conclusions to a certainty within her field:

> Nestle Pure Life bottle (Q21): The DNA profile was a mixture of at least two individuals, but the

major component was a match to the profile of Eric Matthew Frein.

Cigarette butt (Q30): The profile obtained from the cigarette butt found in the Jeep was a single source match to the profile of Eric Matthew Frein.

Black hooded sweatshirt stain (Q44): A stain cut from the back of the sweatshirt yielded a single source match to the profile of Eric Matthew Frein.

Norinco rifle (Q65): The swab from the rifle's trigger, trigger guard, and bolt handle yielded a mixture of at least two individuals, with the major component being a match to the profile of Eric Matthew Frein.

Rifle magazine/rounds (Q68): The swab from the magazine and eight rounds yielded a mixture of at least two individuals, with the major component being a match to the profile of Eric Matthew Frein.

Force quantified the significance of the match: the probability of randomly selecting an unrelated individual with the same DNA profile was approximately one in 8.4 quintillion in the Caucasian population—a number followed by 18 zeros. Unimaginative odds.

THE BALLISTIC MATCH

Pennsylvania State Police Corporal Joseph M. Gober, a certified expert in firearm and tool mark examination, confirmed that the Norinco semi-automatic rifle (Exhibit 414), chambered in 7.62 x 51 millimeter, was fully functional and the murder weapon.

Gober compared a test-fired round (M148) with three evidence bullets found at the scene: the bullet fragment recovered from the soffit (Exhibit 497/J3), the bullet fragment collected from the lobby floor (Exhibit 501/J4), and the bullet recovered from the tree across Route 402 (Exhibit 500/J5). Gober confirmed that all three evidence bullets were identified as having been discharged from the Norinco rifle.

He also confirmed that all four casings found across from the barracks (Exhibit 65) and the two casings found in the Jeep (Exhibit 122) were identified as having been discharged from the Norinco semi-automatic rifle. The casings and ammunition were stamped "AFF88"—manufactured by Ammunition Factory Footscray, Australia, in 1988.

The evidence concluded with the final, binding forensic connections: Monte Swank (FBI Latent Prints) identified all three latent prints recovered from the tape on the pipe bomb components as matching the known prints of "Eric Matthew Frein." Travis McCrady (FBI explosives examiner) confirmed that the components found were fully and partially assembled IEDs. Susan Marie Marvin (FBI metallurgist) confirmed that the wire found in the hangar was consistent with coming from the same spool.

The Commonwealth's presentation of evidence was complete, having established both the chemical and personal authorship of the explosive materials, and the physical link of the murder weapon to the man in the navy blue suit.

THE HOME AND THE TOOLS OF AMBUSH

The inquiry then shifted from the woods to the domestic quiet of 308 Seneca Lane, the house where the plan had been incubated. Trooper David Brodeur of the Special Emergency Response Team (SERT) described the entry as a "slow and deliberate clear," a tactical invasion of a suburban home that revealed a bedroom turned into a shrine of intent.

Corporal David Andreuzzi and Trooper Sandra VanLuvender cataloged the inventory of a mind preparing for war. On the bottom shelf of a bookcase, they found the manual *Sniper Training and Employment*. It was a text that stripped murder of its emotion and reduced it to geometry and physics, defining the sniper's mission as delivering "precise rifle fire from concealed positions."

But it was a yellow legal pad, lying innocuously on a table, that dissolved any remaining illusion of impulsive madness. In handwriting that was terrifyingly mundane, Frein had written a checklist titled "Things to Do."

It was a litany of chores for the apocalypse: "clean Jeep, inspect cache, repack, re-assess equipment, clean guns, re-sight a firm zero."

He listed his needs with the banality of a grocery list: "extra clothes, toiletry kit, food, H2O, radio, batteries, cookware." And then, at the end of the list, a single, jarring word that hinted at the human frailty beneath the soldier's posture: "sleepy."

Nearby, on a desk, sat the chemistry of the bombs: containers of Hodgdon Pyrodex and Goex Black Powder, a mortar and pestle stained with residue, and a spool of wire—the raw ingredients of the devices that would later be found in the woods, waiting for a footfall.

THE MAN WHO WOULD NOT DIE

The Pike County Courthouse, a sturdy Victorian pile of red brick and granite, sat indifferent to the spring light washing over Milford. Inside, the air was stale with the accumulation of ten days of testimony, the atmosphere thick with the peculiar, suspended tension that accompanies the dismantling of a human life.

On this morning, the 17th of April, the jury was not asked to look at the bloody havoc of the crime scene, nor the shattered bones of the victims. Instead, they were invited to peer into a more sterile, yet perhaps more chilling abyss: the electronic catacombs of Eric Frein's mind.

The witnesses were not men of passion but technicians—excavators of the digital soul.

First came Michael Gownley, a retired state trooper with the quiet demeanor of a librarian, who had received the two thumb drives found in the abandoned hangar. He was followed by Derek Fozard, an expert in the silent language of binary code. Fozard's task was to act as a medium, pulling the "digital ghost" of the defendant out of the ether and into the harsh fluorescent light of the courtroom. He had parsed the deleted files, the browsing history, the electronic detritus that modern men leave behind like footprints in wet cement.

What emerged from the hard drives was a portrait of cold, meticulous obsession.

The laptop, it turned out, was a mirror in which Frein had spent years admiring his own grim reflection. The jury learned of his search queries, typed into the Bing search engine with the patience of a spider spinning a web: "Honesdale Pa. Police," "Newfoundland Pa. Police," "Hawley Pa. SWAT." These were not idle curiosities; they were the localized coordinates of a hunter seeking his quarry.

Most damning were the searches conducted on the very day of the murder, September 12, 2014. While the rest of the world went about its ordinary business, Frein was studying the playbook of his enemies, accessing websites with titles like "the post shooting procedures, Police Firearms Officers Association" and "the communication center response to officer down calls."

He was choreographing the aftermath before the first shot was even fired.

And then, the ghost began to watch itself. The forensic examination revealed that during those 48 days in the wilderness, while helicopters beat the air above him and dogs strained at their leashes, Frein was huddled over his screen, tracking his own notoriety. He searched for "Blooming Grove barracks," for "instructions on how to delete a Facebook page," and, with a narcissism that bordered on the pathological, for "Eric Frein" and "Bryon Dickson." He even visited his own Wikipedia page, checking the entry for the capital charges and the $175,000 reward on his head, verifying his status as a national villain as one might check a stock ticker.

But it was a temporary file, a digital scrap titled simply "temp.rtf" and dated October 6, 2014, that stripped the defendant of his soldier's armor. It was a letter—a suicide note, really, composed by a man who had not the courage to die, addressed to the parents whose home he had fled.

Fozard read the text into the record, and the voice that filled the courtroom was not that of a revolutionary, but of a lost and frighteningly small child calling out from the dark:

"Our nation is far from what it was and what it should be. I have seen so many depressing changes made in my time that I cannot imagine what it must be like for you. There is so much wrong and on so many levels only passing through the crucible of another revolution can get us back the liberties we once had. I do not pretend to know what that revolution will look like or even if it would be successful."

The letter continued, attempting to frame his crime as a grand geopolitical gesture: "Tension is high at the moment and the time seems right for a spark to ignite a fire in the hearts of men. What I have done has not been done before and it felt like it was worth a try."

Then, the grandiose language crumbled into the mundane logistics of burial: "If I am dead I would like to be buried in a wood casket (no lead lined casket!) so that my remains can return to where they came from. I realize that this may not be possible though, laws and what not, so don't sweat it. Also, light a candle for me at the Russian or Greek Orthodox church in Stroudsburg from time to time."

Finally, the apology, stark and devastating in its simplicity: "I am sorry. You guys are great parents, I am just not a good son. I squandered so much opportunity and support and rarely tried my best at anything. God knows I do not deserve the things I had, maybe He knew I would be sacrificing all of it in the end, or maybe this is just the final squander. Who knows. I love you. Please forgive me of my many faults. And thanks for putting up with me for so long."

SELF-PORTRAIT IN HANDWRITING

Mark Gardner, a forensic document examiner, approached the stand to perform a different kind of autopsy, one of ink and loops. His task was to bind the prisoner to the "ambush narrative," the three crumpled, mold-stained pages found in the garbage bag at the campsite.

Gardner led the jury through the microscopic landscape of Frein's penmanship. He projected enlargements of the letters, pointing out the "fine and subtle details" that act as a fingerprint of the subconscious. He showed them the word "and," with its distinctive "pointy bottom" on the "a" and the flat top of the "d." He traced the specific architecture of the word "didn't," noting the angular apostrophe and the break between the "n" and the "t."

There were no dissimilarities, he concluded. The hand that had written the checks for the parents' bills was the same hand that had written, with chilling detachment, "He dropped and yelled. I was surprised at how quick."

Following him came Julia Barker of the Secret Service, a chemist of paper. She testified that the crumpled pages from the trash and the notebook found in the hangar were not merely similar; they were siblings. They shared the same 11 spiral-binding holes, the same dimensions, and under the chemical gaze of thin-layer chromatography, the optical brighteners in the paper were "indistinguishable." The science confirmed what the narrative suggested: the memoir of the murder had been torn from the book of the man.

THE LAST KIT OF
CORPORAL DICKSON

The trial, now in its relentless tenth day, abandoned the woods for the chill of the morgue and the austere light of the forensic laboratory. The day was given over to the Commonwealth's final, grim accounting.

Trooper James Hitchcock approached the stand, bringing with him the cold optics of the killer. He testified that he had gone to the ambush site just the night before to recreate the gaze of the assassin. Using the IOR Valdada scope found in the hangar—the very glass Frein had looked through—he took a photograph from the "wooded area across the street."

A Valdada scope is a high-end rifle scope manufactured by IOR (Întreprinderea Optică Română) in Bucharest, Romania, and imported into the U.S. by Valdada Optics in Texas. This instrument provided Frein with a tool that allowed a massive range of internal adjustment, perfect for the job at hand.

The resulting image was a study in vulnerability. It showed the front doors of the barracks framed perfectly within the optics, the "V" of the trees acting as a frame, the reticle's red illumination set to "one." It was the view of a predator, static and unblinking.

Then, Pennsylvania State Police Corporal Joseph Pericci laid bare the final effects of the fallen man. He produced Corporal Dickson's duty belt—a harness of authority holding his Taser, his mace, his handcuffs. He described the Glock Model 21 pistol, fully loaded with 12 rounds in the magazine and one in the chamber, a weapon that had never cleared its holster.

The items were laid out, the heavy, tactile tools of a man prepared for a confrontation that never came, a man who had been erased from the world before he could even reach for the defense at his hip.

THE CLOSING ARGUMENTS

Settled after ten days of absorbing the stark horror presented, the jury was brought in to hear the final appeals to reason and conscience.

District Attorney Ray Tonkin advanced to the jury box, his voice dark and resonant with the finality of the state's vengeance. He began by reciting the killer's own narrative, reproduced by the Associated Press and reprinted by its affiliates. "A terrorist with murder in his heart, a plan in his mind, and a rifle in his hands slithered through the woods under the cover of darkness on September 12, 2014." He demanded the crime be recognized for its true nature: "literally hunting humans." He cited Frein's own letter, "…only passing through the crucible of another revolution can get us back to the liberties we once had," to prove the specific intent . He detailed the agonizing, deliberate nature of the crime, demanding the jury recognize the "minute and a half" Frein waited between shots, a "lifetime" in the woods "waiting to shoot somebody else."

Tonkin demanded that the full weight of Frein's journal be accepted as his confession of purpose. He used the devastating lines from Frein's journal, telling the jurors they were "chilling beyond imagine," and that Frein's words— "Another cop approached the one I just shot. As he went to kneel, I took a shot at him and he jumped in the door. His legs were visible and still"—were "something only the perpetrator of this crime could have written down." He pointed to the Norinco rifle with its Romanian model scope designed to measure human distance, arguing that Frein had executed the crime with "the precision of a military operation." He concluded that Frein's choice to change government with "bullets and bombs" was nothing less than terrorism.

The Norinco, in its cheap, stamped-steel reality, was an unlikely instrument for such a savage ballet of fate. It was not a precision tool, not a Winchester or a Remington, but a crude, almost brutish thing, mass-produced in some distant, anonymous factory. Its wood stock was of indifferent quality, the bluing thin, already showing the faint patina of neglect, perhaps a touch of rust where the fingerprints had lingered too long. It had the grim, utilitarian aesthetic of something designed for a purpose far removed from sport or ceremony; it was made to spit lead, nothing more.

One imagined it smelling of solvent and stale gun oil, a faint, metallic tang that clung to the hands. When loaded, its weight shifted, becoming substantial, no longer a mere object but a loaded intent. The bolt, though not smooth as silk, cycled with a decisive *clack*, chambering the round with an unceremonious certainty. The trigger, often gritty, would eventually break, sending the slug on its path.

This particular Norinco, however, had transcended its humble origins. It had become a character in a ghastly play, imbued with the cold purpose of its wielder. It had absorbed the tension of the long wait, the breath held, the world narrowed to a crosshair's precise intersection. It had felt the tremor of human hands—not in fear, but in the dreadful anticipation of decision.

And then, twice, it had spoken. Not with a roar, but with a sharp, concussive crack that tore the quiet night, each utterance a final, irrevocable judgment. It had launched its copper-jacketed messengers into the darkness and, in their wake, it had left behind a terrible, echoing silence, punctuated only by the fading throb of human hearts and the cold, unfeeling whisper of the wind through the Pennsylvania pines. The rifle itself remained impassive, an inert piece of metal and wood, oblivious to the havoc it had wrought, waiting, perhaps, for its next chilling command.

Tonkin opened for the Commonwealth with the kind of methodical precision that had characterized both the investigation and his own approach to criminal prosecution throughout his career. Standing before the jury box in his dark suit and burgundy tie, his tall frame commanding the courtroom's attention, he spoke in the measured tones of a man who understood that the most effective advocacy often comes not from theatrical flourishes but from the careful presentation of facts.

"Ladies and gentlemen of the jury," he began, his deep voice carrying easily to the back of the courtroom, "on the night of September 12, 2014, at approximately 10:50 p.m., Corporal Bryon K. Dickson II stepped out of the Pennsylvania State Police barracks in Blooming Grove Township to begin his shift. He was thirty-eight years old. He was a husband and the father of two young boys. He had served his country as a Marine and his community as a state trooper for seven years. He had every reason to believe that he would complete his shift, return home to his family, and continue the life of service that had defined his adult years."

Tonkin paused, allowing the weight of those words to settle over the jury before continuing. "What Corporal Dickson could not know—what he had no reason to suspect—was that for months, perhaps years, the defendant had been planning his murder. Eric Matthew Frein had transformed himself into an instrument of violence, had selected the Blooming Grove barracks as his target, had positioned himself in the woodland with a high-powered rifle, and had waited with the patience of a predator for the moment when he could strike."

The prosecutor moved across the courtroom with deliberate steps, his hands clasped behind his back, his eyes never leaving the jury. "The evidence will show that this was not a crime of passion, not a moment of anger or fear that spiraled out of control. This was premeditated, calculated murder—what the law defines as first-degree murder. The defendant planned this crime. He prepared for this crime. He executed this crime with the precision of a military operation. And when he was finished, Corporal Dickson was dead and Trooper Alex Douglass lay bleeding on the pavement, his hip and pelvis shattered, his life forever changed."

The opening statement continued for nearly 40 minutes, as Tonkin methodically outlined the evidence that would prove Frein's guilt beyond any reasonable doubt. He spoke of the ballistics evidence that would link the bullets fired at the barracks to the ammunition found in Frein's abandoned vehicle. He described the extensive manhunt that followed, the 48 days during which an entire region lived in fear while Frein evaded capture in the Pennsylvania woodland. He promised testimony from surviving victim Alex Douglass, from the officers who had responded to the scene, from the investigators who had methodically assembled the case against the defendant.

"At the conclusion of this trial," Tonkin concluded, his voice carrying the full weight of prosecutorial authority, "you will have heard evidence that establishes beyond any reasonable doubt that Eric Matthew Frein is guilty of the premeditated murder of Corporal Bryon K. Dickson II, of the attempted murder of Trooper Alex Douglass, and of terrorism—the use of violence to intimidate a government agency and the citizens it serves. The evidence will be clear, it will be compelling, and it will demand a verdict of guilty on all charges."

The defense response, when it came, carried the kind of resigned professionalism that marks attorneys who understand the impossible nature of their task. Michael Weinstein rose from the counsel table with the deliberate movements of a man who had spent decades in criminal courtrooms, his tall frame unfolding as he approached the jury with the careful steps of someone navigating treacherous terrain.

"Ladies and gentlemen," Weinstein began, his voice carrying none of the prosecutorial certainty that had marked Tonkin's opening, "I will not stand before you and tell you that Eric Frein is innocent of these charges. The evidence against him is, as Mr. Tonkin has said, overwhelming. What I will ask you to consider, as this trial progresses, is the question of why—why a man with no prior criminal record, a man who had lived thirty-one years without violence, would commit such acts."

It was a strategy born of desperation disguised as reasoned analysis—an attempt to transform a case about premeditated murder into an inquiry about the social and psychological forces that can transform an ordinary citizen into a killer. Weinstein spoke briefly about the evidence that would emerge regarding Frein's mental state, his increasing isolation from mainstream society, his descent into an ideology that viewed law enforcement as an occupying army rather than public servants.

"We do not ask you to excuse what Eric Frein did," Weinstein concluded. "We ask only that you consider all of the evidence, all of the circumstances, as you deliberate on the appropriate verdict in this case."

Attorney Michael Weinstein, speaking for the defense, began with an acknowledgement of the "tragedy of monumental proportions" that had taken place. His posture was defensive, mournful, and respectful of the impending storm. He stressed the "great pillars of American justice"—the presumption of innocence and the unyielding burden of proof beyond a reasonable doubt. Though he "certainly acknowledged that that mountain of evidence" pointed directly at his client, Eric Frein, he asked the jury to decide whether "that gap between pointing and proof beyond a reasonable doubt has been satisfied." He recalled the inexplicable delay in finding the Jeep—"not discovered by either of those aircraft" for "some three days"—and the ominous fact that the campsite was "ransacked" before being photographed. He closed with the quiet insistence that they draw "no adverse inferences" from Eric Frein's failure to testify, a silence guaranteed by the Constitution.

District Attorney Ray Tonkin countered with a final, searing narrative of calculated ruin, delivered in the language of the murderer's own planning. He began with the now-infamous opening: "A terrorist with murder in his heart, a plan in his mind, and a rifle in his hands slithered through the woods under the cover of darkness on September 12, 2014." He insisted the jury follow the path of evidence where it led, because the man who committed this act "sits right over there." He cited Frein's own chilling manifesto—"Our nation is far from what it was and what it should be... only passing through the crucible of another revolution can get us back to the liberties we once had"—and called it "the words of the real Eric Matthew Frein." He hammered the concept of specific intent required for the two counts of first-degree murder. He pointed out that under the law, this intent did "not require planning" and "can happen in the snap of a finger."

He then detailed the agonizing, deliberate nature of the crime, demanding the jury recognize the 90-second wait between the second and third shots, a "lifetime" in the woods for the killer to wait for his next victim. He used the devastating lines from Frein's journal—"Another cop approached the one I just shot. As he went to kneel, I took a shot at him and he jumped in the door. His legs were visible and still"—as unassailable proof of specific intent to kill Trooper Douglass. Tonkin concluded that Frein's plan, from the sniper scope "used to measure the distance to and to shoot humans" to his deliberate disregard for PCO Nicole Palmer, proved he was "literally hunting humans," and that his choice to "change it with bullets and bombs" was nothing less than terrorism.

THE LAW'S UNYIELDING GEOMETRY

Judge Gregory H. Chelak then delivered the final instructions. His charge was a long, solemn lecture on the law's cold geometry, defining the legal framework that would govern the jurors' judgment.

He defined malice not as hatred, but as the "mental state that the law regards as being bad enough to make a killing murder." First-degree murder required "willful, deliberate, and premeditated," including "by means of lying in wait." He instructed that flight or concealment was a "circumstance tending to prove the person is conscious of guilt" but cautioned that the jury "may not find the defendant guilty solely on the basis of evidence of flight or concealment."

The judge meticulously detailed the elements of all 12 counts, including criminal attempt (requiring a substantial step); terrorism (requiring an intent to influence the policy of a government); weapons of mass destruction (defined as a bomb, biological agent, chemical agent, or nuclear agent); and recklessly endangering (for PCO Palmer, if the defendant "consciously disregards a substantial and unjustifiable risk"). He informed them that if they found Frein guilty of attempted murder (Counts 3 and 4), they must determine if the attempt resulted in serious bodily injury to Alex Douglass. Finally, he reminded them that "you must not draw any inference of guilt or any other inference adverse to the defendant from the fact that he did not testify at this trial."

The jury retired to deliberate at 12:49 p.m. After deliberating for over four hours, the Court reconvened at 5:06 p.m. The bailiff confirmed the jury had reached a verdict, and the foreperson rose to read the 12-step verdict slip, their voice steady.

The evidence against Eric Frein was overwhelming, that much became clear within the first hour of deliberations. The DNA, the ballistics, the videotaped confession in which he sat smoking cigars and describing the murder with the casual precision of someone discussing a recipe. James Morrison, the paper mill supervisor, had summarized it best: "We're not here to decide if he did it. We're here to decide what it means that he did."

But it was during the penalty phase that Margaret Kowalski felt the full weight of what they were being asked to do. She had listened to Tiffany Frein describe her brother as her protector, had watched the mother Deborah Frein break down on the witness stand, had seen the father—that strange, broken man—admit to teaching his son that the police were the enemy. And she had thought of her own children, grown now with children of their own, and wondered what failures of love and guidance might transform a quiet boy who earned his Eagle Scout badge into a man who could wait in the woods with a rifle, patient as a hunter, and shoot another human being in the back.

The deliberations stretched into evening. Sarah Chen, the young accountant, had argued passionately for life imprisonment, citing the documented abuse in the Frein household, the father's alcoholism and violence. But others on the jury—particularly the men—had focused on the premeditation, the 48 days of evasion, the pipe bombs discovered in his possession. One juror, a retired Marine, had said simply, "He hunted them. He hunted cops like they were animals."

When they finally voted, it was unanimous for the death sentence. Margaret had cast her ballot last, her hand trembling slightly as she marked the paper. In her 37 years of teaching, she had learned that children were infinitely malleable, that the right intervention at the right moment could redirect an entire life. But she had also learned that there came a point when the clay hardened, when the choices made could not be unmade, when the only response to certain acts was to remove the actor from the world entirely.

She thought of Corporal Dickson's widow, sitting in the gallery day after day, her face a mask of controlled grief. She thought of Alex Douglass, walking to the witness stand on his prosthetic leg, his entire future reduced to a catalog of surgeries and permanent limitations. And she thought of her own grandchildren, playing in their suburban yards, innocent of the darkness that could erupt without warning into the most ordinary of nights.

When the foreperson read the verdict aloud—death by lethal injection—Margaret felt no satisfaction, no sense of justice served. Only an immense weariness, and the knowledge that she would carry this decision with her for whatever years remained. That evening, she would return to her farm, to her husband of 43 years, and she would not speak of what had happened in that room. Some burdens could not be shared, only endured.

The answer, delivered with absolute, chilling unanimity, was Guilty, on all twelve counts.

For Count 1 (Murder of the First Degree) and Count 2 (Murder of a Law Enforcement Officer of the First Degree), the verdict was Guilty. The attempt against Alex Douglass (Counts 3 and 4) was also found Guilty, and the jury affirmed "Yes" to the question: "Did the defendant's criminal attempt result in serious bodily injury to the victim, Alex Douglass?"

The charge of Assault of a Law Enforcement Officer (Count 5) was Guilty. For the two counts of Terrorism (Counts 6 and 7), the verdict was Guilty, with the jury affirming, line by line, that the underlying violent offenses included First-Degree Murder, Murder of a Law Enforcement Officer, Criminal Attempt (all categories), and Assault of a Law Enforcement Officer. The possession of Weapons of Mass Destruction (Counts 8 and 9) was also Guilty. Finally, the acts of Discharge of a Firearm Into an Occupied Structure (Count 10), Possessing Instruments of Crime (Count 11), and Recklessly Endangering Another Person for PCO Nicole Palmer (Count 12) were all found Guilty.

At the request of the defense, the 12 jurors were polled individually, each confirming, one by one, their agreement to the verdict. The jury's duties, the Court informed them, were "not yet complete," as the penalty or sentencing trial—the terrible calculus of death—would begin the following afternoon at 1:30 p.m. The Court remanded Frein to the Pike County Correctional Facility until the next session. The long, terrible wait was over; the final, unanimous judgment had been rendered.

The Commonwealth, having presented its final, unanswerable evidence—the killer's planning, the victim's demise, and the cold scientific certainty of the ballistic match—had no further questions. The testimony concluded with the formal stipulation that both Corporal Bryon Dickson II and Trooper Alex Douglass were law enforcement officers. The Commonwealth rested. The defense, having mounted no evidence, rested as well. The meticulous and terrible calculation was finished, leaving the judgment to the 12 citizens of the jury.

The 11th day of the trial, April 19, 2017, arrived not for the grim introduction of new evidence, but for the final, terrible synthesis of all that had been seen and heard. The long road of evidence—the bloody sidewalks, the cold computer code, the voice of the wounded—had led the courtroom to this single, irrevocable hour: the rendering of the law's judgment.

The session began in the small, quiet sanctum of chambers, where the lawyers performed their final legal rites before facing the jury. Mr. Tonkin stood with the Commonwealth's final, meticulous requests, confirming the last stipulation: that the man referred to throughout as Bryon Dickson was, by solemn agreement, Bryon K. Dickson II, as listed on the official indictment. The Commonwealth also finalized the charges for terrorism, agreeing to "eliminate" certain paragraphs from the indictment that were not specifically tied to the shooting acts. Judge Gregory H. Chelak noted the amendments to his own final charge, explaining to counsel his intention to slightly alter the instruction on malice, defining it simply as "the mental state that the law regards as being bad enough to make a killing murder." All was now complete. The vast, complex machinery of the law was ready to deliver its final, simple truth.

THE CONTRADICTIONS
OF THE CONDEMNED

The defense, shouldering the crushing weight of the jury's unanimous verdict of premeditated murder, dedicated the morning to populating the defendant's desolate interior landscape with threads of human connection and mitigating virtue. They called a series of witnesses who attempted to paint Eric Frein not as the cold-blooded terrorist of the woods, but as a man of quiet, dependable competence who had simply become disastrously derailed.

The penalty phase offered the defense their only real opportunity, and Michael Weinstein had approached it with the grim determination of a man trying to bail out a sinking ship with a teaspoon. He had called Frein's family to the stand—the mother with her desperate, rambling testimony about abuse and learning disabilities, the father who had lied about being a Vietnam veteran, the sister who described Eric as her childhood protector. He had hired experts to testify about the effects of childhood trauma, about the psychology of anti-government extremism, about how a person could be simultaneously functional and profoundly damaged.

But the prosecution had been relentless. Ray Tonkin, the district attorney, had stood before the jury during closing arguments and methodically dismantled every mitigating factor they had presented. The abuse? Other children from troubled homes did not become cop killers. The isolation? Frein had made choices, deliberate choices, to withdraw from society and nurse his grievances. The political ideology? A convenient excuse for premeditated murder.

When the jury returned with their verdict—death—Weinstein felt no surprise, only a deep exhaustion that seemed to settle into his bones. He had known, from the moment he was assigned the case, that this was how it would end. Pennsylvania juries did not hesitate to impose death sentences on cop killers, particularly when the crime was as calculated and cold-blooded as this one.

That night, alone in his office in Milford, Weinstein poured himself a bourbon and reviewed the trial transcripts, searching for grounds for appeal. It was a ritual he performed after every death sentence, this archeological expedition through the debris of a concluded case, looking for the procedural error, the constitutional violation, the single reversible mistake that might save his client's life.

He found nothing. Judge Chelak had been scrupulously fair, the jury instructions proper, the evidence properly admitted. The system had functioned exactly as designed, grinding slowly and inexorably toward its predetermined conclusion. Eric Matthew Frein would die by lethal injection, and there was nothing Michael Weinstein or anyone else could do to prevent it.

He thought, not for the first time, about finding a different line of work. Corporate law, perhaps, where the stakes were merely financial. But he knew he would not leave. Someone had to stand between the defendant and the machinery of the State, even when—especially when—the defendant was guilty, unrepentant, and utterly unsympathetic. It was the price of calling oneself civilized, this insistence that even monsters deserved representation.

Weinstein finished his bourbon and began drafting the notice of appeal. It would be denied, of course. They always were. But that was not the point. The point was to make the system work for its verdict, to force the State to jump through every hoop, satisfy every requirement, cross every procedural "T" and dot every constitutional "I." If they were going to kill Eric Frein, they would do it according to the rules, with every safeguard in place, every option exhausted.

It was cold comfort, but it was the only comfort available in this particular line of work.

Afterall, the defense faced an impossible task.

The narrative began with the quiet efficacy of his military life, a portrait sketched by his former supervisors. Sergeant Derek Felsman, Frein's former supervisor in the Army Reserve, testified that Frein was "very quiet" and utterly "professional," an "excellent soldier" who performed his duties "without failure." This image of quiet, reliable efficiency was immediately reinforced by Lieutenant Colonel Joseph L. Grealish, Frein's former commanding officer, who affirmed that Frein was a "very quiet individual" and "very competent in his job." The defense sought to argue that Frein's martial skill, though tragically misapplied, originated in discipline and order, not inherent chaos or malice.

The cornerstone of the entire defense strategy, however, was the cold, unblinking assessment of Dr. Robert Johnson, a criminologist and prison expert. After reviewing Frein's prison records and interviewing his family, Dr. Johnson—a specialist whose expertise touched on the grim reality of life behind walls—testified about the crucial legal concept of future dangerousness. He offered the clinical assessment that inmates sentenced to life without parole generally pose "no risk or low risk" to staff and other inmates. Frein's profile, he concluded, matched this low-risk category, noting that he was "well-educated" and had exhibited "no history of violence within the jail." This testimony was the final, reasoned plea for life, arguing that the killer's capacity for violence was extinguished once he was permanently and humanely confined; that the State's interest in finality could be met without the ultimate, irrevocable sentence of death.

VICTIMS' REBUTTAL

The defense's carefully constructed framework of mitigation was met with the unwavering, piercing grief of the victim's family, who spoke not of abstract policy or psychological profile, but of the irrefutable, permanent emptiness left in their lives.

Bryon Dickson Sr., the murdered trooper's father, took the stand for the Commonwealth's rebuttal. His testimony was a powerful validation of his son's lost life. "He was a man of integrity, he was a son of integrity." He spoke of the "devastation" of the family's loss and the unceasing, absolute pain.

Darla Dickson, Corporal Dickson's mother, followed, her words echoing the high military creed that had defined her son. She noted that Corporal Dickson was a man of "honor, service, and integrity," values he had lived out as a Marine and a Pennsylvania State Trooper. Her testimony focused on the agonizing, unchangeable present tense of their grief. The family, she insisted, "cannot laugh" and "cannot move on," their lives forever defined by the unfillable void left by Frein's crime. Their quiet grief was the final, unanswerable evidence.

The Court, having heard the complete, harrowing evidence of both the crime and its profound human cost, the methodical logic of the defense, and the broken hearts of the victims' parents, adjourned for the weekend. The jury was left to weigh the chilling efficiency of the killer's competence against the permanent ruin he had inflicted. The terrible act of life and death would resume the following Monday.

The trial resumed its glacial progress on Monday, April 24, for the grim second act of the penalty phase. Having failed to secure an acquittal, the defense was now engaged in the desperate, profound exercise of establishing mitigating factors—searching for the hidden humanity in a man who had committed an act of calculated, inhuman malice. The courtroom, stark in its official severity, became a confessional where the family of the convicted murderer offered their fractured narratives as a final, fragile defense against the sentence of death.

THE FATHER: A LEGACY OF QUIET GRIEF

The defense's mitigation began with Eugene Michael Frein, the defendant's father, a man whose presence carried the unspoken weight of a flawed inheritance. Mr. Weinstein sought to quickly establish the core of a quiet, if peculiar, life. Mr. Frein confirmed that his son, Eric, was "very close" to his mother and him, describing him as "loyal" and a "very kind and a loving boy" who was nonetheless "very, very quiet." The father testified to Eric's early promise as an Eagle Scout and his love for the outdoors, often engaging in camping and hiking. He recalled Eric's vast interest in military history and his meticulous devotion to model railroads. Critically, Mr. Frein established the family's martial bona fides: Eric owned an enormous arsenal—"twenty-five rifles, nineteen handguns, two shotguns"—and confirmed he had personally taught his son gun safety, with father and son often enjoying "going to the range" together.

The prosecution, through Pike County First Assistant District Attorney Bruce DeSarro, quickly navigated the cross-examination to the fatal contradictions. Mr. Frein offered a different phrasing when asked if he himself had told the FBI that "the police were too strong," a sentiment that provided a chilling context for the crime. He was forced to admit he was "aware of his Serbian uniform" and his son's paramilitary interests, though he claimed ignorance of the political website Eric ran. The most agonizing admission was his own visceral reaction upon hearing news of the shooting: "God, that's Eric." He affirmed that he was later compelled to call the police to report the weapons cache, hoping his son would be safely apprehended.

In a rare moment of undeniable good introduced into the record, the defense called Warren Ahner, Eric Frein's childhood best friend. Ahner lived in Silicon Valley, California, where he worked as a software engineering manager. Ahner said he and Eric had bonded over their shared love of computers and the fact that they were both self-described "loners."

THE MOTHER: THE SCARS OF HOME

Debbie Frein, Eric's mother, followed, her testimony a desperate plea against finality. She described Eric as "always a quiet kid" and "very sensitive." Like his father, she remembered his time as an Eagle Scout and his preference for "solitary activities" like reading. The defense then delicately introduced the domestic ruin that had shaped the killer: Mrs. Frein confirmed that Eric's father, Eugene Michael Frein, was abusive toward the children and her. Eric, she testified, was "very protective" of his sister, Tiffany, during those dark moments. She spoke of a later incident when Eric dropped out of college in 2004 after meeting a professor whose wife was killed in a school shooting, a trauma that deeply affected her son and provided a terrible new layer to his subsequent obsession with firearms. She confessed that Eric had only "snapped out" of his long-standing moodiness in the hours before the ambush, acting "normal" immediately prior to his final departure.

Attorney Tonkin, in cross-examination, systematically dismantled the defense's mitigating framework with the weight of the physical evidence. Mrs. Frein was forced to confirm the damning inventory of the Frein residence: the two IEDs discovered in the basement, the sniper manual and ammunition in his bedroom, and the purchase of the .308 caliber rifle and Glock Model 21 were documented. She admitted that Eric belonged to the Red Alliance, wore the Serbian uniform, and held a firm dislike of the police. Tonkin read from the letter found on the computer, ensuring the mother acknowledged her son's own words that provided the political justification for his act: "I have seen so many depressing changes made in my time that I cannot imagine what it must be like for you." The effect was devastating: Debbie Frein's raw, personal mitigation was met by the unyielding, documented reality of her son's premeditation.

Jason Haller, a childhood friend who had known Eric since 1999, offered the final, brief plea for the man he once knew. Haller confirmed Eric was "never loud," "very introverted," but reliable and "a good person." He never witnessed any violence from him. The defense, having presented the full, difficult portrait of familial dysfunction, quiet competence, and ultimate pathology, submitted its mitigating evidence. The case now rested on whether these broken personal truths could outweigh the cold certainty of the two first-degree murders.

The Pike County Courthouse, a place of stolid brick and unforgiving routine, became, on that morning of April 25, 2017, the stage for the peculiar, heartbreaking spectacle of a murderer's mitigation. The Honorable Gregory H. Chelak presided, a man attempting to impose order upon a narrative that had long since surrendered to chaos. The lawyers—

Tonkin and DeSarro for the Commonwealth, Ruzzo and Weinstein for the defense—were present, engaged in a cerebral, often acrimonious dance of legal maneuvering, all centering on the slight, silent figure of Eric Matthew Frein.

The day's proceedings, the continued penalty phase hearing, began not in the full, anxious view of the jury, but in the judge's chambers, where the grim business of restricting truth commenced. The Commonwealth, represented by Attorney Tonkin, moved to bar the testimony of a woman named Louise Luck, whom the defense sought to parade before the jury as a mitigation expert. Tonkin, with a prosecutor's weary skepticism, cast the expert as a mere vessel for "a bunch of hearsay"—an "end run around the Hearsay Rule." He pointed out that Ms. Luck had apparently prepared no formal report, offering only a vague letter, and suggested that her intended testimony merely duplicated evidence already placed before the jury, subject to the proper cross-examination that she would evade.

In reply, Attorney Ruzzo argued that Ms. Luck, a former probation officer with a master's degree in community psychology, was a seasoned professional, having conducted "forty-two to forty-three interviews with family members and others." Her expertise lay in uncovering "family history," which Ruzzo insisted carried "a certain indicia of reliability" and was necessary to frame the defendant's case for life under the auspices of the Sixth and Eighth Amendments. The battle was less over Ms. Luck's bona fides than over the defense's strategy: Ruzzo was attempting to weave a grand, multi-generational tapestry of hardship and contributing factors, while Tonkin fought to trim it back to the verifiable, cross-examinable facts.

The Court ultimately arrived at a judicial compromise: Louise Luck would be allowed to testify, if properly qualified as a "mitigation expert." Her testimony, however, would be tightly bridled—she could speak to her role, disclose facts she reasonably relied upon "to support her opinions and not to the truth to the underlying matter," and the jury would be given a precise, limiting instruction. As the judge dryly noted, her allowance would not be a "carte blanche to testify as to every single case of hearsay." She would be confined to the "four corners of the letter" already disclosed to the Commonwealth.

With the legal scaffolding thus erected, the curtain rose on the defense's mitigating testimony. The first witness was Jeremiah Hornbaker, an art director for film and television, who spoke of his loose, professional acquaintance with Eric Frein. Hornbaker had hired Frein in 2009 for a nine-day documentary film project for the U.S. Marine Corps Museum—a simulated Battle of Belleau Wood. Frein, apparently, proved capable in his role doing "greens work," helping with landscaping and assisting Marines with "their weapons training and safety." Hornbaker characterized him as a "reliable" and enthusiastic employee, good at his job, and trustworthy enough to provide "accurate information" concerning the period detail crucial to the work. However, the witness confirmed that this direct employment was confined to that single nine-day period nearly a decade earlier, and that to the best of his knowledge, Frein had "never served in the United States military." The defense seemed to suggest a capable, hard-working man; the Commonwealth underscored the lack of substance behind the military pretense.

Next, the jury heard from the defendant's adoptive sister, Tiffany Frein, a young woman who would turn 21 that June, and whose testimony provided the first lacerating glimpses into the domestic heart of the Frein family.

The girl—though at 20 she was technically a woman—sat in the witness box with the peculiar stillness of someone who has learned that any sudden movement might provoke violence. Her hands were folded in her lap, neat and small, and she kept her eyes fixed on the defense attorney who had called her to testify, as if looking anywhere else might cause her to dissolve entirely.

Tiffany Frein had spent most of her life trying to be invisible. It was a survival skill learned early in the household on Seneca Lane, where her father's rages erupted without warning and her mother's protections proved unreliable. Eric had been the only constant, the only person who stood between her father's fists and her face, and now she was being asked to reconcile that Eric—her protector, her hero— with the Eric who had shot two police officers and spent 48 days hiding in the woods like an animal.

She had not visited him in jail. The lawyers had explained that such contact might be misinterpreted, might suggest some kind of coordination or shared ideology. But the truth was simpler and more painful: she did not know what she would say to him. The brother who had once pulled her into his room and distracted her with card games while their father raged downstairs had become someone she no longer recognized, someone capable of waiting in the darkness with a rifle, calculating angles and distances, patient as death itself.

The defense attorney was gentle with his questions, coaxing from her the stories of childhood abuse that she had spent years trying to forget. She described her father grabbing her by the hair and throwing her to the ground, calling her names that no father should speak to a daughter. She described the door broken off its hinges, the fist connecting with her face seven times, the metallic taste of blood and terror. And through it all, she described Eric—quiet, serious Eric— telling their father to leave her alone, offering her sanctuary in his room, creating a small, protected space in a house that had never felt like home.

"He was my protector," she told the jury, and her voice broke on the word. It was perhaps the truest thing she had ever said, and also the most complicated. Eric had protected her, had shielded her from violence, but he had also absorbed that violence himself, had internalized it and transformed it into something else entirely—a hatred that extended beyond their father to encompass all authority, all government, all men in uniform who represented the system that had failed to protect them both.

She understood, in a way the jury probably could not, that Eric's crime had its roots in that house, in those years of learned helplessness and rage. But she also understood that this explanation was not an excuse, that thousands of children survived abuse without becoming killers, that the line between victim and perpetrator was one that Eric had chosen to cross.

When the prosecutor cross-examined her, his questions were sharp and skeptical, designed to undermine her testimony by revealing its incompleteness. Yes, her brother Michael had grown up in the same household and had not become a murderer. Yes, she herself had experienced the same abuse and had channeled it into nursing, into helping rather than destroying. The implication was clear: Eric's choices were his own, not products of their shared trauma but deliberate decisions for which he bore full responsibility.

After her testimony concluded, Tiffany left the courthouse through a side entrance, avoiding the cameras and reporters who waited for any family member willing to speak. She drove back to her small apartment in Scranton and sat in her car for a long time, unable to summon the energy to go inside. She thought about Eric, sitting in that courtroom in his navy suit, his face empty of expression, and she wondered if he had become empty inside as well, if the years of military reenactments and anti-government ideology had hollowed him out until nothing remained but the performance of conviction.

She would learn to live with this, eventually. To introduce herself without mentioning her last name, to deflect questions about her family, to construct a life separate from the terrible fame her brother had earned. But she would never stop missing the Eric who had been her protector, the quiet boy who had stood between her and violence, even as she condemned the man he had become. This was the particular burden of loving someone who commits the unforgivable: the love does not end simply because the person has become monstrous. It persists, a vestigial ache, a phantom limb that throbs with remembered warmth even after amputation.

Her relationship with Eric, she stated, was one of need and fierce loyalty. "He was my big brother. He was somebody that I looked up to. He was my protector." Her parents, she confessed, were "very abusive towards me," and Eric was the only one who would intervene, shouting, "Leave her alone," or simply offering comfort. "It's okay, Tiff, you know how Mom and Dad are. Just come upstairs and let's hang out."

Tiffany recounted harrowing instances of this abuse: once, her father "grabbed me by the hair and he threw me on the ground, and he made me crawl to my room and called me a little bitch and then slammed the door." On another occasion, after she called her father "an asshole," "he broke down my door and he punched me in the face seven times." It was Eric, she insisted, to whom she turned, the one who "really stepped up to the role." She described her father, who used to come home drunk "with his pants around his ankles," as "angry, very self-centered, ignorant, or arrogant." She herself, due to the fraught family atmosphere, had no contact with her extended family, lamenting, "Technically, to me I don't have a family. I never really did. Eric was my home."

During cross-examination, Attorney Tonkin sought to blunt the impact of her testimony, establishing that her mother was a "manipulator" and confirming that the family had not discovered until the day before that their father's claim of being a Vietnam combat veteran was a lie. Tonkin then confronted her with a police report suggesting Eric "had talked about killing a person that stole a pistol from your house." Tiffany claimed she could not remember this detail, though she recalled a pistol being missing. She was also pressed on Eric's political interests, confirming he believed the Serbian government was "better than ours," but she denied he talked about changing the U.S. government. Tonkin concluded by noting that her other brother, Michael, despite growing up in the "same household," was "gainfully employed in the pharmaceutical industry."

The third defense witness was Ellen Mitchell, Eric's older half-sister and Eugene Michael Frein's biological daughter. Her presence in Eric's life was sparse, limited to a year of living with his family in 1984 when Eric was almost two, and periodic visits when the family lived in Indiana up until she graduated high school, followed by a single weekend ski trip in 2006. She characterized the home's environment during her one-year stay as "stagnant," testifying she "knew that I wasn't wanted" by her stepmother.

However, her most devastating testimony focused on the father she shared with the defendant. She revealed that in the years leading up to 2006, her father, when he would call her, "would call me drunk," talking about "his marital affairs, how much he disliked his wife," and toward the end, he "talked about wanting to kill people. Just any people. He had a rage inside of him." She relayed this observation to

Eric during their 2006 ski trip, and Eric "said that Dad drank a lot." The Commonwealth attempted to block her from offering her reaction to reading a statement by her father—"My son shoots great. He doesn't miss"—on the grounds that her interpretation would be speculation and hearsay.

Following Ellen Mitchell's brief tenure on the stand, the defense rested its case, after the formality of Eric Frein's colloquy. Sworn in, the defendant confirmed on the record that his decision not to testify was "voluntary, knowing, and intelligent," made with the advice of counsel, and that he understood the jury could draw "no adverse inference" from his silence.

The afternoon brought the Commonwealth's rebuttal. They called two witnesses, attempting to undermine the defense's narrative of Eric Frein as a lost soul with poor prospects and a dysfunctional family.

Kim Barrow, a senior employment practices partner from AstraZeneca, testified that Eric M. Frein had "no" records of employment at their facility, countering any unstated notion of pharmaceutical industry work.

The next witness, Geryl Kinsel, the associate registrar at East Stroudsburg University, detailed Frein's academic record, or lack thereof, producing his official transcript. The records showed that Frein never received any degree. Kinsel highlighted Frein's academic performance in 2005: The spring semester resulted in grades of B, B, D, and C, and the fall semester culminated in "E"s, which "are failing grades." The record was conspicuously blank between 2005 and 2008, and after the spring of 2012, there were no further records of his attendance. Kinsel also presented copies of refund checks, with Frein's signature acknowledging receipt, totaling over $4,600 across late 2011 and early 2012, hinting at financial aid disbursements. The checks, the

Commonwealth suggested, were another form of support the defendant had received, even while failing to complete his education.

Finally, Kathleen Cronin, an accounts clerk from the Pike County Correctional Facility, authenticated a compact disc containing a recording of a visitation call made by the defendant on November 19, 2014. Over the defense's objection, the Commonwealth played a portion of the call where Frein discussed selling his story, mentioning "media inquiries" and indicating that "he would not speak until the end of the trial," after which he would be "asking for money and then uses the term, highest bidder." This, the prosecutor argued, was potent rebuttal to the mother's "character endorsement" and spoke to Frein's "rational person" status, which was critical to their penalty phase arguments. A second recording, from April 2017, where Frein allegedly dismissed the defense's mitigation strategy as an attempt to make him "appear to be a nut job," was ultimately suppressed by the judge, who expressed concern over using the defendant's own words—a legal strategy that could easily provide grounds for an appeal.

With the testimony for the day concluded, the lawyers and the judge retreated to chambers for an extensive conference on jury instructions. The Commonwealth, among other requests, asked that if their expert, Dr. Eric Zillmer—who had interviewed the defendant and prepared a report on the psychology of terrorists—was not allowed to testify, the jury should be instructed to disregard Mrs. Frein's "unresponsive outburst" that her son was "delusional" and her plea that his life be spared. The judge decided to review Dr. Zillmer's report and either allow his testimony or instruct the jury to disregard the specific, volunteered comments by the mother.

The last order of business was the "Life is Life" instruction, where the Commonwealth vigorously objected to the standard wording telling the jury they could "assume" the governor or Board of Pardons would act "responsibly" and not commute a life sentence if they believed the prisoner was "dangerous." This, the prosecution argued, was asking the jury to make a baseless "assumption" in violation of common legal practice. The defense countered with its own proposed instructions, one focusing on the lack of required "nexus" between mitigating circumstances and the crime, and another, directly quoting a prior case, that would explicitly permit the jury to consider "sympathy or mercy" as a reason to impose a life sentence. All of these requests and arguments would await the judge's final decision, ensuring that the morbid calculations of the penalty phase would continue the next morning.

The morning unfurled with the grim ritual of the penalty phase, transforming the courtroom into a stage for the delicate, often agonizing drama of a man's final fate. The first voice to be heard belonged to Jeremiah Hornbaker, whose connection to Eric Frein was entirely professional and rooted in a singular, distant film project: a nine-day documentary for the Marine Corps in 2009.

Following this professional sketch, the proceedings devolved into the deeply personal territory of the Frein home, delivered by Tiffany Frein, the defendant's 20-year-old adoptive sister. Her testimony drew the picture of a household corroded by abuse, in which her brother Eric emerged as her singular anchor, her "protector." In a rush of painful revelation, she recounted her father's brutal behavior and Eric's staunch refusal to tolerate it. "Why don't you leave her the hell alone. All you people do is go after her and make her feel like she's less than nothing."

The final voice for the defense was that of Ellen Mitchell, Eric's half-sister, whose knowledge of the family's interior life was geographically and temporally strained, rooted in only a single year of cohabitation when Eric was an infant, and occasional, later visits culminating in a ski trip in 2006. Yet, she added a profound and chilling stroke to the family portrait, revealing that in the years preceding the crimes, her father's drunken phone calls escalated into angry confessions: he "talked about wanting to kill people. Just any people. He had a rage inside of him."

The Commonwealth's rebuttal then sought, in its own hard-edged way, to dismantle the defense's gentle framing, summoning two witnesses to establish Frein's lack of professional and academic success. Geryl Kinsel, the East Stroudsburg University registrar, produced the cold, damning truth of the defendant's academic record, attesting that Frein "never received any degree" and spotlighting semesters marred by "failing grades" and long stretches of non-attendance. Similarly, Kim Barrow of AstraZeneca stated plainly that Frein had "no" record of working for the pharmaceutical company. The Commonwealth concluded its presentation by calling Kathleen Cronin, an accounts clerk from the Pike County Correctional Facility, who authenticated a recording of Frein from detention, a piece of evidence which, once played, was meant to portray him not as a pitiful product of circumstance, but as a coolly "rational person" discussing the commercial sale of his story to the "highest bidder" after the conclusion of his trial.

The arguments put forth by the lawyers, stripped of their courtroom ceremony, were stark calculations concerning a man's fate and the meticulous rules governing what the jury was permitted to know. The initial, crucial skirmish revolved around Louise Luck, the defense's purported mitigation expert, whom the Commonwealth's Attorney Tonkin sought to silence. With the weary precision of a man determined to prevent sentiment from poisoning justice, he dismissed her proffered testimony as nothing more than a lawyer's clever maneuver—an "end run around the Hearsay Rule"—designed to sneak inadmissible, uncross-examinable gossip before the jury. He argued that she lacked a proper report, offering merely "a letter," and that all her usable facts had already been "testified to" by other witnesses, thus making her testimony merely "cumulative" and her role superfluous.

The defense, led by Attorney Ruzzo, countered with a grander, more philosophical appeal to fairness. He argued that Ms. Luck, with her master's degree and her "forty-two to forty-three interviews," was a necessary guide for the jury, entitled to present the multi-generational sorrows and family history that comprised the defendant's context. Ruzzo invoked the solemn authority of the Sixth and Eighth Amendments, asserting that the defense was obligated to present its full case for mercy, and that the history Ms. Luck compiled carried an "indicia of reliability" that superseded the narrow, "mechanistic Hearsay Rule." The Court, in an act of cautious compromise, allowed her testimony but chained it with strict limitations: she could not testify as to the truth of the underlying facts, but only disclose information reasonably relied upon "to support her opinions," and she was sternly admonished not to offer "carte blanche to testify as to every single case of hearsay."

A second, more volatile confrontation centered on the Commonwealth's desire to use rebuttal testimony to refute the emotional, unbidden outburst of the defendant's mother, Debbie Frein, who had declared her son "delusional" and pleaded with the jury to "not sentence her son to death." The prosecution wished to call Dr. Eric Zillmer, a neuropsychologist whose expertise included the pathology of terrorists. This testimony, Tonkin insisted, was necessary to rebut Mrs. Frein's layperson declaration, thereby restoring the narrative of a calculated, rational murderer whom the doctor could confidently categorize. Ruzzo dismissed the mother's comment as mere layman's opinion, arguing that calling an expert to combat a single word blurted by a parent was a gross distortion of the rebuttal function. The judge, caught between the mother's raw, tearful plea and the Commonwealth's cold, scientific counterattack, postponed his ruling, announcing he would either allow the psychiatrist's testimony or "give an instruction to the jury to disregard the specific areas"—the mother's plea and the mention of delusion—to keep the balance of the scales even.

Finally, the lawyers tussled over the delicate language to be used in the jury's final instructions, particularly the "Life is Life" charge. The Commonwealth, ever vigilant against the intrusion of speculation, vehemently opposed the standard language that invited the jury to "assume" that the governor or the Board of Pardons would not commute the sentence of a dangerous prisoner. This instruction, they argued, was asking the jury to wade into the "wilderness of what they can assume" based on "no evidence," a dangerous and unwarranted invitation to speculation that threatened the integrity of their verdict.

We must now turn from the dark inheritance of the family to the equally barren ground of the murderer's ambitions, detailing a meager academic career as thin and unpromising as a faded photograph.

THE FINALITY OF THE VERDICT

The jury's path to the death sentence was paved by their unanimous and absolute acceptance of all aggravating circumstances presented, a judicial fact that left no avenue for mercy to creep in.

These findings, proven beyond a reasonable doubt, provided the legal scaffolding for the execution order.

The murder was aggravated by the fact that the victim, Corporal Bryon K. Dickson II, was a peace officer or state law enforcement official killed in the performance of his duties or as a result of his official position.

Furthermore, they found the defendant committed the killing while in the perpetration of several felonies related to the criminal attempt to commit murder of a law enforcement officer (Trooper Alex Douglass).

The verdict was also based on the commission of the killing during the perpetration of felonies involving terrorism and the use of weapons of mass destruction.

The intentionality was underscored by the knowing creation of a grave risk of death to additional persons, specifically Trooper Alex Douglass and PCO Nicole Palmer, during the commission of the offense.

The jury also affirmed the felony of discharge of a firearm into an occupied structure (the Blooming Grove barracks), and the fact that Frein was also convicted of another State offense of murder of a law enforcement officer in the first degree (the other count) committed at the same time.

The jury's total acceptance of every aggravating circumstance and its simultaneous rejection of every single mitigating factor submitted by the defense ensured the verdict was mandated as death under Pennsylvania law.

THE HAMMER OF JUSTICE

The jury, in its swift and final reckoning, returned the ultimate sentence of death on both counts of murder. The chilling core of their verdict was the unanimous finding of no mitigating circumstances and the affirmation of all aggravating circumstances presented by the Commonwealth. This wholesale rejection of the defense's plea for mercy rested on the overwhelming weight of the following factors, proven beyond a reasonable doubt.

Amid the legal precision, the Court was compelled to provide the jury with instructions on the difficult, ephemeral concepts of sympathy and mercy, a necessity born from years of constitutional rulings. The Court first gave the standard instruction that the sentence "must be in accordance with the law... and not be based on sympathy, prejudice, emotion, or public opinion." This instruction functions as a general guardrail against arbitrary passion.

Crucially, however, the Court instructed the jury that it was "entirely proper" to consider "sympathy or mercy as a reason to impose a life sentence."

This mercy, however, was not to be mere sentiment. The judge carefully stressed the limitation: this sympathy or mercy "must be founded upon any item or items of evidence any one or more of you find to be a mitigating circumstance." In essence, mercy could only be entertained if it flowed directly from the specific, proven mitigating facts presented by the defense.

The final instructions gave each juror the freedom to find a mitigating circumstance even if others did not, thus allowing any single juror's finding of a mitigating factor—such as the tragic family history or Frein's childhood difficulties—to serve as the foundation for a vote for mercy. By finding no mitigating circumstances whatsoever, the jury effectively removed the entire foundation for granting mercy, sealing Eric Frein's fate.

The defense, in its attempt to conjure a picture of a man deserving of mercy, offered a long, sprawling list of nearly 30 mitigating factors. The Court, however, trimmed this list with sharp judicial shears, often finding the proposals either unsubstantiated by evidence, argumentative in nature, or overly vague.

The first and most significant strike came against the claim that the "Defendant has no significant history of prior criminal convictions," a factor the defense had utterly failed to support with any evidence. As the Commonwealth pointed out, and the defense was forced to concede, there was "no evidence at all" put forth during the sentencing hearing regarding Frein's criminal history, leaving this proposed mitigating factor entirely baseless. Under the law, a mitigating factor must at least be supported by some evidence, and this one was not.

Many of the remaining proposals were challenged for their excessive repetition, their argumentative language, or their sheer lack of factual support.

For instance, the claims that "Eric was embarrassed to be called out by teachers for help" or that the father, "Eugene Michael Frein had a long-term problem with alcohol" were challenged as not being properly supported by the evidence or as placing argumentative language into the mouth of the Court. Similarly, the argument that "Eric was isolated from extended family members" was accepted only after a lengthy debate, given that the testimony supporting this factor was focused on the family as a whole, rather than the defendant's personal, deliberate isolation.

The defense's long list of separate arguments—that the Frein household was "angry," that the parents had "serious marital problems," or that the father "was ready to snap at any time"—were largely viewed by the Court as argumentative language that would be consolidated into broader, non-argumentative categories on the official verdict slip.

The fate of a number of other factors rested on narrow evidential points.

The statements that Frein had a "learning disability" or "could not read on his own until the sixth grade" were included, but only as factual claims that the jury would have to weigh against the lack of corroborating school records or official documentation. Conversely, the statement that Frein "babysat for niece and nephew" and was "Godfather to nephew"—small acts of decency amid the darkness—was accepted as a proper mitigating factor.

It wasn't just an absence of school records that doomed this mitigating factor; it was the prosecution pointing out the glaring contradiction that a man with a supposedly crippling reading disability was studying advanced ballistic trajectory and military tactics.

The claim that Frein "expressed remorse for his offenses and concern for the victim's family" was also allowed to stand, despite the Commonwealth's vigorous objection, forcing the jury to weigh this brief display of emotion against the cold evidence of Frein's calculated planning. Ultimately, the Court took the multitude of raw, sometimes confusing assertions, and consolidated them into the most accurate, concise language possible, ensuring that the final list presented to the jury—which ultimately rejected every single point—was a disciplined, legally coherent catalog of the circumstances offered for mercy.

We now come to the cold, hard figures of Eric Frein's meager academic career, a final, pathetic detail used by the Commonwealth to argue for his chilling rationality and competence.

The Commonwealth presented the testimony of Geryl Kinsel, the associate registrar from East Stroudsburg University, to precisely detail Frein's academic shortcomings and the financial dividends of his failure. It was proven that Frein never received any degree from the institution. He was not merely a student; he was an economic actor in the educational system.

Frein's record showed that despite the failing grades and periods of non-attendance, he successfully received thousands of dollars back from the university in the form of refund checks—money presumably derived from student loans or financial aid for which he was briefly eligible. This cold transaction was meant to contrast sharply with the defense's narrative of the "broken boy," revealing instead a man capable of manipulating institutional bureaucracy for personal gain.

The specific, documented amounts Frein obtained from the university were as follows:

September 29, 2011: $1,441.11 (fall 2011 semester).

Spring 2012: $995.37.

Spring 2012: $344.74.

February 29, 2012: $1,850.00.

These funds, totaling $4,631.22, were not the reward of academic achievement but the consequence of enrollment and withdrawal, signed for personally by Eric Frein himself. The money represented a final, verifiable fact: even in his half-hearted attempt at a professional life, Frein was capable of calculating a financial advantage, an "accurate information" exchange meant to refute any suggestion of comprehensive delusion or mental incompetence.

THE MARATHONER

To understand what was stolen from Trooper Alex Douglass, one must first understand what he was. In the years before the bullet found him, his body was not merely a vessel, but an instrument of precision and endurance. He was an ultra-marathoner, a man who measured his worth in miles and elevation gain. He had run 50 miles through the rugged terrain of the North Face Endurance Challenge, pushing past the point where the lungs burn and the muscles scream, into that silent, rhythmic fugue state where the mind detaches from the pain and floats.

Running was his meditation, his religion. It was the architecture of his days—the early morning training runs, the careful calibration of diet and rest, the singular focus on the next finish line. He was a man defined by motion, by the power of his own legs to carry him across vast distances.

And then, in a fraction of a second, the architecture collapsed.

The bullet from Eric Frein's rifle did not just break bone; it shattered identity. It entered the lower back and tore through the pelvis, exploding the right hip and femur before exiting. In that instant, the runner died and the patient was born.

THE LONGEST MILE

The recovery was not a journey; it was a siege. Douglass spent months in a hospital bed, his world reduced to the four walls of a sterile room and the rhythmic beeping of monitors. The man who had once run through forests for joy was now trapped in a body that could barely lift itself.

The pain was a constant, unwelcome companion. It was not the clean, honest burn of a long run, but a jagged, nerve-shredding agony that defied medication. Phantom sensations haunted him—the ghost of a stride he could no longer take, the twitch of muscles that had been severed.

Physical therapy became his new marathon, but the milestones were agonizingly small. Lifting a leg a few inches. Standing for a minute without passing out. Taking a single, faltering step with a walker. Each victory was hard-won, paid for in sweat and tears, and each one served as a cruel reminder of how much had been lost.

But the physical pain was only half the battle. The mental darkness was a deeper, more insidious enemy. For a man whose self-worth was tightly tied to his physical prowess, the loss of mobility was a kind of spiritual amputation. He watched his legs, once strong and defined, wither from disuse. He felt the pity in the eyes of visitors, the unspoken acknowledgment that he was broken.

There were days when the darkness threatened to consume him, when the memory of the runner he used to be felt like a taunt. He would close his eyes and see the trail stretching out before him, feel the wind in his face, the rhythm of his breathing—and then open them to the harsh reality of the wheelchair and the colostomy bag.

THE DECISION

Four years. Four years of surgeries—18 in total. Four years of infections, of rods and pins, of hope raised and dashed. Four years of trying to save a leg that had become a prison.

The right leg, the one that had been shattered, remained a source of constant torment. It was a dead weight, a painful anchor that kept him tethered to that night in September. He could not run. He could barely walk. He was trapped in a limbo of chronic pain and limited mobility.

And then, Alex Douglass made a decision that required a courage far greater than running fifty miles.

He decided to cut it off.

It was not a surrender; it was a liberation. He realized that the leg was not him. It was just flesh and bone, and it was holding him back. To regain his life, he had to lose a part of himself.

On December 12, 2018, in a hospital in New York City, surgeons removed Alex Douglass's right leg below the knee. The .308 speck of mass destruction that had traveled a circuitous route though his body had robbed his lower extremity of the vital blood flow to support the limb.

When he woke up, the pain was different. It was the clean pain of healing, not the rotting pain of injury. And for the first time in four years, he felt a flicker of the old fire.

THE REBIRTH

The prosthetic leg was not a replacement; it was a tool. Carbon fiber and titanium, cold and hard, but responsive. Douglass learned to walk again, then to run. It was awkward at first, a staccato rhythm unlike the fluid stride of his youth, but it was motion.

He returned to the gym, to the weights, to the sweat and the effort. He found a new community in CrossFit, surrounded by others who understood the language of pushing limits. He was no longer the broken trooper; he was an adaptive athlete.

In 2022, he stood at the starting line of the New York City Marathon. He was not running it; he was hand-cycling, using the strength of his arms to propel himself through the five boroughs. But he was there. He was in the arena.

At the same time, Eric Frein sat in a cell, his world shrinking with every passing day, his "revolution" reduced to the four walls of death row. He had destroyed himself for a delusion.

Alex Douglass, the man he had tried to break, rebuilt himself. He lost a leg, but he found something stronger: an indomitable will that refused to be defined by what was taken, but by what remained. He is still an ultra-marathoner, not because of the miles he runs, but because of the distance he has traveled from the darkness back into the light.

THE ARCHITECTURE OF PAIN

If Bryon Dickson was the silence of the grave, Alex Douglass was the scream of the living. He had survived, a word that suggests triumph but felt, in the early days, like a different kind of sentence.

The bullet had done more than break bone; it had rearranged his reality. He lay in a hospital room that smelled of antiseptic and stale flowers, a white box where time was measured not in hours but in the intervals between doses of morphine. The silence here was different than the silence in the woods. It was the mechanical silence of machines breathing for you, of fluids dripping through tubes, of a body that had become a stranger to its owner.

Eighteen surgeries.

The number is easy to say, but the reality is a grinding attrition. It is the repeated violation of the flesh in the name of healing. Surgeons replaced his hip with titanium, rebuilding the architecture of his pelvis like engineers shoring up a collapsing bridge. He lay there, a young man in the prime of his physical life, now trapped in a wreckage of scar tissue and atrophy, staring at the ceiling tiles and asking the unanswerable question: *Why him and not me?*

Survivor's guilt is a parasite. It feeds on the "what ifs." If he had walked out the door a second later. If he had turned left instead of right. If the wind had blown differently. He carried the weight of Dickson's death in his own shattered hip, a heaviness that no physical therapy could lighten.

Then came the training. The marathon was not a race; it was an exorcism.

The first time he tried to run, it was an act of grotesque difficulty. His body, once fluid and capable, rebelled. The pain was sharp and electric, a warning signal from nerves that had been severed and reconnected. But he ran. He ran with a limp that was a testament to the violence he had absorbed. He ran through the fear of loud noises, the PTSD that turned a slamming door into a gunshot, the sudden panic that gripped him when the wind moved the trees in a certain way.

Putting the uniform back on was the hardest mile. The gray wool was no longer just clothing; it was a target. To wear it was to invite the crosshairs back into his life. But he did it. He stood in the mirror, adjusting the tie, smoothing the fabric over the scars, and he saw a man who had been disassembled and put back together—different, harder, but still standing.

THE LAWYERS' TALE

The transcript lay on the table like a dissected animal, each page another layer of flesh peeled back, the organs, questions, objections, and rulings, pinned and labeled in a neat, black-ink hand.

The room where it was read was not the courtroom, not the stage of oaths and glances and solemn nods, but a quieter annex of the same drama: a small, lamplit place where one person turned pages while another, unseen, had already turned their life over to the State.

In the trial proper, the story had been simple enough to memorize. A bad act, a bad actor, a procession of voices who swore they had seen, or heard, or intuited the truth.

But the transcript told a different story. It recorded every stuttered "um," every polite "yes, sir," every time the judge's patience thinned to a single word—"sustained"— and in those interruptions, in the ragged edges that never reached the evening news, the case took on a different shape. What looked, from the gallery, like an orderly march toward justice revealed itself, on paper, as something more fragile: a human attempt to corral memory, pain, and fear into the narrow grammar of the law.

The lawyers moved through this landscape like practiced surveyors, their questions forming invisible fences around pieces of the past.

One of them, the prosecutor, favored short, clean sentences, a carpenter of yes-or-no answers who seemed allergic to ambiguity. The other, for the defense, preferred longer loops—questions that began at childhood and wound their way, through bad luck and worse decisions, to the day of the crime.

Between them, the defendant emerged not as a single, solid figure but as two incompatible silhouettes: in one telling, a calculating figure moving toward an inevitable harm; in the other, a person gradually pushed toward a final, terrible misstep.

If the lawyers were the architects of this narrative house, then the judge was the quiet building inspector, his influence more visible in what could not be seen.

The record showed moments when the jury was led out, the heavy door closing behind them, and the voices in the room changed. Polite tones became sharper; legal phrases—"unduly prejudicial," "outside the scope"—began to appear, like warning signs along a mountain road. From these sidelong arguments, whole branches of the story vanished. A statement was struck, a photograph excluded, a rumor never allowed to rise to the dignity of evidence. To read those pages was to watch a second trial, conducted in the shadow of the first: the trial of what the jury would be permitted to know.

It was in these gaps, these carefully curated silences, that the true stakes of the case announced themselves.

One afternoon, a witness began to say more than the question called for, about a night long before the crime, about a house with thin walls and shouting that seemed to go on until morning. There was an objection, brisk and almost embarrassed, as if someone had walked into the room half-dressed. The judge conferred in low tones, the jury absent. In the end, the past was trimmed down to a single, harmless sentence.

The rest remained in the transcript like a ghost, visible only to those who came afterward and read the whole record, not just the official story.

The penalty phase, when it arrived, did not feel like a continuation so much as a change in weather.

The same courtroom, the same walls and worn carpet, but the light had shifted. The questions turned inward: childhood, sickness, the peculiar geometry of a life that had led here and nowhere else. Witnesses who had once described acts now described wounds. A teacher spoke of a boy who never raised his hand but flinched when the door closed too loudly. A sibling recalled long car rides, the parent's hands tight on the wheel, the silence in the back seat thicker than any argument. Listening to them, one had the sense of an invisible ledger being rewritten—not erasing the crime, but surrounding it with so much prior pain that the neatness of guilt began to blur at the edges.

Still, the prosecution's theme persisted: some lives, they suggested, carry their own verdict.

Their questions were careful to steer the story away from gray areas. Had the defendant not chosen, again and again, to cross lines plainly marked? Had there not been help offered, chances given, warnings issued? They spoke of the community, the need for safety, the "message" that would be sent by anything less than the harshest punishment. In their hands, the penalty phase was not a second story but an epilogue to the first, a final chapter whose ending had been written long before the jury filed in.

The defense saw it differently.

To them, this was the first time the whole person stood before the court. They lingered on small, almost domestic details: a favorite book at the age of 12, a job that had briefly gone well, a quiet habit of washing dishes long after everyone else had gone to bed. In their telling, the same chronology the State used as a staircase to condemnation became a chain of missed opportunities and unhealed injuries.

They did not deny the act; instead, they tried to widen the frame until the single, terrible moment seemed less like a solitary choice and more like the last tile in a long, complicated mosaic.

Throughout all of this, the witnesses formed a kind of chorus, each voice distinct yet somehow part of the same song.

Reading the transcripts, one noticed how certain words reappeared—as if passed around the room like a shared cup. "Afraid," one said. "Confused," said another. "Tired," said a third, talking not of that night but of the years before it. Their testimonies overlapped and contradicted, not in ways that suggested lying, but in the ordinary way that human beings misremember according to their own fears and loyalties. When arranged side by side, they did not cancel each other out. They produced, instead, a three-dimensional picture of a tragedy nobody saw from every angle at once.

Beneath the words, beneath the tidy columns of questions and answers, there was also the record of the room itself.

The notations—"(witness crying)," "(laughter)," "(pause)"—told their own story. A joke, made perhaps to loosen a tight-lipped witness, landed awkwardly enough to provoke a brief, nervous chuckle. A long silence stretched between a question and its answer, the type of silence that, in person, would have been filled with the sound of someone swallowing hard or staring at their hands.

When the judge noted, "Let the record reflect that the witness is visibly upset," the phrase was, in its way, both precise and heartbreakingly vague.

What did "visibly upset" look like? A trembling lip? A jaw clenched in fury? The transcript did not say. It trusted that those present would remember. It did not anticipate that, one day, the paper itself would become the only surviving witness.

And always, at the margins, the jury.

"Jury enters," "jury exits"—a ritual, repeated until it lost all novelty for the clerks who typed it, but whose significance never quite dimmed. The roomful of citizens who knew only what they were allowed to know, who saw only the version of events that had survived the objections and the sidebars and the solemn calculations of admissibility. They were the intended audience of the performance the trial had become, yet the least articulate presence in the record. They never spoke, except sometimes in aggregate—"the jury appears attentive," "the jury has reached a verdict"—and yet everything hinged on what they made, privately and without stenographic assistance, of what they had heard.

To sit with the complete transcript is to occupy a vantage point denied to everyone present at the time.

The lawyers, trapped in their strategies, could not step back; the witnesses, imprisoned in their own memories, could not compare their stories to those of others; the jurors, barred from half the conversations, could not see how much had been trimmed away before the case was handed to them. Only later, in that quiet room where pages turned and the past was no longer a moving picture but a stack of paper bound with a thin blue cover, did the full complexity reveal itself.

The trial, once admired for its clean lines and clear conclusion, began to look more like what it always had been: a human attempt, earnest and flawed, to fix in words something that never stopped moving.

STATE OF DOMESTIC TERRORISM

The landscape of American terror has shifted, much like the changing seasons on the vast, silent stretches of the American interior—subtle at first, a crispness in the air, until the frost sets in hard and deep. It is no longer the specter of foreign planes or coordinated cells from distant lands that haunts the national slumber. Instead, the threat has turned inward, becoming a domestic creature, born of the soil and the silence of American living rooms.

In the mid-20s of this new century, the menace is not a singular, thundering storm, but a pervasive, lingering fog. It is the "lone offender," a figure as solitary and inscrutable as a drifter of the old sort, yet drifting now through the digital highways rather than the forgotten county roads. These men—and they are, principally, men, often terribly young— sit bathed in the blue light of computer screens, their faces slack, minds feverish with a cocktail of grievances. They are the primary architects of this new unease.

The Federal Bureau of Investigation, that great cataloger of human frailty, has noted a distinct evolution. By the close of 2025, they were chasing some 1,700 ghosts—active domestic terrorism investigations that spanned the breadth of the continent. The danger now arises from a "confluence of factors," a bureaucratic phrase that hardly captures the venom involved. It is a mix of racially motivated animus and anti-authority rage, a simmering stew where the political right and the anarchic left occasionally bleed into one another, united only by a desire to see the structures of society burn. The year 2024, with its bruising election cycle, acted as a kind of accelerant, pouring gasoline on embers that had been glowing quietly in the dark.

One observes a disturbing trend in the geography of this violence. It does not always seek out the grand monuments of the capital. It prefers the "soft targets"—a term of chilling bureaucratic efficiency. It seeks the grocery store in a quiet neighborhood, the house of worship during morning prayers, the power station humming alone in a thicket of pine. The intent is to disrupt the mundane, to shatter the very ordinary peace that allows a citizen to buy a quart of milk or bow their head in prayer without the expectation of death.

There is, too, a specific focus on the machinery of the State. Law enforcement officers, once the unquestioned guardians of the peace in these rural and suburban enclaves, find themselves in the crosshairs, viewed by the "sovereign citizens" and militia men not as protectors, but as the enforcement arm of a tyrannical beast. The rhetoric is apocalyptic, the actions sporadic but lethal.

Statistically, the numbers rise and fall, but the feeling of the threat remains high. The Department of Homeland Security (DHS) speaks of a "heightened threat environment," a persistent anxiety that hangs over the country like the humidity before a storm. The radicalization is rapid, often invisible to the families sleeping just down the hall. A teenager in a bedroom in Ohio or Oregon can be conscripted into a war of hate without ever leaving his chair, his mind warped by algorithms that feed him a steady diet of antisemitism and accelerationism—the idea that society is beyond saving and must be pushed into collapse.

It is a tragedy of isolation. Just as the quiet facades of suburban homes often conceal the desperation within, the digital clutter of modern America hides its own monsters. They are waiting, these solitary figures, nursing their perceived wounds, waiting for the moment to turn their private nightmares into public reality, leaving the rest of the country to wonder, with a mournful shake of the head, how such coldness could bloom in the heart of the heartland.

FOLLOWING A LEGACY

Meanwhile, the village of Blooming Grove sits quiet in the Pennsylvania Poconos, a landscape of dense timber and darker hollows where the sun struggles to touch the forest floor. It was here that Eric Matthew Frein, a man of 31 who still lived in the shadow of his parents' roof, decided to wage a private war. To understand the architecture of his mind, a cluttered attic of military fantasy and silent grievances, one must look not just at him, but at the ghosts who walked these woods before him. He was not a singularity but a variation on a tragic, distinctly American theme: the solitary man who mistakes his own quiet desperation for a call to arms.

Consider, first, the ghost of Eric Rudolph. Like Frein, Rudolph was a creature of the wilderness, a man who viewed the tangled roots and limestone caves not as scenery, but as a fortress. Both men possessed that peculiar, survivalist vanity—the belief that they were smarter than the hounds baying at their heels. In 1998, Rudolph, the bomber of Centennial Olympic Park in downtown Atlanta, the scene of the 1996 Summer Olympics Games, vanished into the Appalachian spine of North Carolina for five years, subsisting on acorns and theft, driven by a rigid, puritanical hatred of the government. Frein, too, fancied himself a master of the terrain, a "ghost" in the Poconos. They shared a psychological kinship found in the patience of the hunter; they were men who could lie still in the dirt for days, waiting for the "enemy"—the uniformed men of the State—to drift into their crosshairs. For both, the woods were their comfort zone. The figure that emerges from the shadows to stand beside Eric Frein—a brother in silence, if not in soul—is Eric Robert Rudolph.

To understand one is to hold a mirror to the other, though the reflection is distorted. Both were men who turned their backs on the warmth of the lighted window to embrace the cold indifference of the American wilderness. Both were "ghosts" who transformed undulating forests into private kingdoms where the laws of men held no currency. But where Rudolph was a creature of granite and fanaticism, Frein was a creature of plastic and performance.

Consider the similarities, for they are striking. Both men chose the rifle and the bomb as their instruments of dialogue. Both harbored a curdled resentment for the government, a vague and sprawling hatred that viewed the badge of a police officer not as a shield but as a target. Rudolph, who spent five years vanishing into the Nantahala National Forest, and Frein, who spent 48 days in the Poconos, shared a tactical arrogance. They believed that the land belonged to them, that they could outwait and outwit the helicopters that buzzed like angry hornets overhead. They both paralyzed communities, turning ordinary autumn nights into seasons of dread, where a snapping twig sounded like a gunshot.

However, the contrast—ah, there lies the tragedy.

Eric Rudolph was a true believer, a man carved from the hard wood of the "Christian Identity" movement, a member of the Army of God, a Christian terrorist organization. His violence was an extension of a terrifying, if coherent, theology. He was an ascetic who lived off acorns and salamanders, a man who could endure the crushing solitude because he believed himself to be a soldier in a holy war. He was, in his own terrible way, authentic.

Frein, by comparison, was an actor who forgot that the curtain had fallen. He was not a soldier; he was a reenactor. He did not wear the fatigues of a cause he lived; he wore the uniform of the Army of Republika Srpska, a costume for a war that had ended when he was a child. He called himself "Vuchko," a borrowed name for a borrowed life. While Rudolph was stealing vegetables to survive a winter, Frein was found with ramen noodles and a thumb drive, keeping a journal that read less like a manifesto and more like a screenplay he hoped someone would find.

Rudolph was a mountain man; Frein was a boy playing in the woods. Rudolph's silence was the silence of discipline; Frein's silence was the sulking of a child who felt the world had not paid him his due respect. When the end came, Rudolph was caught dumpster diving, still fighting to survive. Frein was caught near a rotting honeymoon resort, surrendering without a shot, the "Vuchko" mask slipping to reveal a frightened man with a scratch on his nose, waiting for the applause that never came.

One was a fanatic; the other, a phantasm. But in the end, they both walked out of the woods, the only place they felt truly large, truly powerful, in handcuffs, leaving behind nothing but broken families and the wind moving through the trees, indifferent to them both.

Then there is the shadow of Christopher Dorner, who committed a series of killings in California in 2013. While Frein draped himself in the aesthetics of Eastern European militias—a sort of deadly dress-up—his motive was closer to the raw, festering wound of the former LAPD officer. Dorner, like Frein, declared a manifesto-driven war on the police themselves. They did not target the politicians or the generals; they targeted the blue uniform, the symbol of the authority they felt had humiliated them. In Frein's letter to his parents, he spoke of "igniting a fire," a desire to spark a revolution. It is the same delusional arithmetic that Timothy McVeigh scribbled in his own mind before the Oklahoma City bombing in 1995: the idea that one act of terrible violence could wake the sleeping masses. But where McVeigh sought to bring down a building, Frein and Dorner sought to hunt men, believing that by spilling the blood of a trooper, they were striking a blow for liberty. It is a terrifying narcissism, to believe one's personal grievances are the weight of history.

And finally, one detects the faint, metallic scent of Ted Kaczynski, the Unabomber who killed three and maimed 23 in his 1978 – 1995 mail bombing campaign. They did not compare in intellect—Frein was no mathematician—but in the profound isolation. Kaczynski sat in his Montana cabin, stewing in a hatred for the modern world, convinced that he alone saw the truth. Frein, in his "spider holes" and bunkers, lived in a similar reality distortion field. He was a man who reenacted battles with friends on the weekends but eventually, the line between the game and the world dissolved. He became the soldier he pretended to be. Like Kaczynski, he believed that he could force the world to listen by making it bleed.

In the end, however, when the dogs closed in and the marshals found him in that abandoned airplane hangar, Frein was not the revolutionary he imagined himself to be. He was cold, he was hungry, and he was small. Just as Perry Edward Smith was revealed to be a frightened child with a shotgun who murdered four members of the Clutter family in Kansas in 1959, Eric Frein was stripped of his woods and his war. He was left with only the terrible silence of what he had done—a silence that connects him, by an invisible thread, to all those other lonely men who sought to fill their emptiness with the sound of a gunshot.

DEATH PENALTY STATUS IN PENNSYLVANIA

As of mid-August 2025, nearly 100 men gaze each day into the dull fluorescence of death row, most housed at SCI Phoenix in Montgomery County and SCI Somerset in Somerset County. The execution chamber at SCI Rockview in Centre County remains pristine, unused, the leather straps of its gurney brittle from disuse and indifference. Female death row is theoretical only—a cold cell at SCI Muncy in Lycoming County awaits any exception, but none has come.

It is true, and it certainly appears true, that the machinery of execution in Pennsylvania has rusted quietly into dormancy. No execution has been carried out in this place since the last century, 1999, and even then, only for volunteers—men so bankrupt of hope or remorse they chose needle over appeal, silence over the clamor of time. The truth is, the State is a relic among its power—retaining the death penalty in statute, enforcing it only in theory, as if the threat of it must suffice where the act will not.

In 2015, a moratorium descended, soft but absolute, upon Harrisburg's imposing rotunda. Governor Tom Wolf's pen suspended death as the price of crime, and every subsequent executive, with a manifest of considerations—inequity, error, cost, and the yawning absence of justice—has maintained it. Josh Shapiro, the governor since 2023, has called not only for the suspension, but for the abolition of the death penalty, imploring the General Assembly to drag the gallows into history's dustbin where, he suggests, it truly belongs.

And so there is stasis. The cell doors close, the numbers are counted—still 94 or 96, depending on the hour, the calendar. Appeals spiral and contract, but the needle does not prick. The men—disproportionately Black, overwhelmingly poor, many the products of failed schools, broken representation— wait in a paralysis not of the body, but of the soul. Many have waited more than a decade; some, a generation.

In this vacant theater of the condemned, the only certainty is uncertainty. The sentences remain written, but the script is never performed. The condemned dream not of the chaplain's steady incantations or the press gathered behind dusty glass but instead, of further appeals, commutation— and perhaps, in the most stubborn hours of the night, hope.

The gurney stands unused, draped always in the institutional anonymity of a system that can countenance murder, but not the sight of its aftermath. Guards walk their rounds with a special detachment, the rituals of death row reduced to the banality of ordinary lockdown. Out in the political darkness, campaigns to abolish the penalty gather signatures and dust in equal measure.

In Pennsylvania, then, death row is less a sentence than a condition—a slow tumbling of days in the humid blankness of cells, suspended above the inferno but not quite free of its heat. The condemned, neither living nor quite dead, become—in a word writers themselves might have relished—the ghosts in the machinery, haunting the corridors of justice long after the world has lost the will to carry out its sentence.

In that narrow corridor of stone and steel, where the hours echo in their passing, where time persists in its slow, sedimentary accumulation, Eric Frein remains. Cut away from the world by distance and by the law, he lives among other men who share his sentence, not by choice or fraternity, but by the cold arithmetic of justice meted out in the Commonwealth of Pennsylvania. Here, at SCI Phoenix, a place as carefully observed as an operating theater and as silent as a tomb, the geometry of his existence has changed, though not the essential gravity.

The days no longer slip past in the solitary, airless dark once prescribed to those who await the State's slow machinery. Reform came, bringing with it new customs: an open door, though only to a walled yard; a voice, though limited by the mechanism of a telephone; a procession to the showers, to the chapel, and sometimes to the sunlit square of concrete called "recreation."

Forty-two and a half hours out, in the communal air, over the course of each week—a freedom that is not freedom at all, but a widening of the cell. Meals now taken in the company of others, each glance and gesture observed, yet there is company, nonetheless.

Conversations pass through the wire, measured in minutes, and the ritual of the daily call becomes both anchor and clock.

Education is offered, and such work as is permitted is labor for the sake of occupation, not advancement. There are visits, sometimes separated by glass, sometimes not, in the visitation room, a place where the world outside makes quiet, brief incursions.

The guards no longer stride with automatic authority, ordering strip searches at each movement or demanding the prisoner be shackled hand and foot for the trivial migration from one threshold to the next. Now such rituals of humiliation are reserved for cause, not as constant hum.

But always there is the fundamental silence of death row, a hush comprised of time, regret, and the unending expectation.

The law in Pennsylvania is paused at the moment between sentence and execution, the moratorium silencing the gallows, yet leaving each man suspended, neither living freely nor finishing the walk that was promised on verdict day.

Eric Frein's days unfold under observation, the body safe from others, the mind left to wander. Yet, in the careful design of reforms and daily rituals, the essential fact persists. There are no open fields, no cool breezes, no sound but the artificial pulse of institution. A man may read, or write, or pray; he may recall the sky as he saw it once—a memory that recurs, perhaps, in the slant of light falling from a distant window. But within these walls, the past is remade only in shadow, and the future remains a cipher.

Thus the world passes, slowly and quietly, in that place, and in that state; his is a sentence of waiting and of being seen, but never quite touched.

In the American landscape, a place of amber waves and asphalt arteries, the term "domestic terrorist" carries with it a certain weight—a label stitched onto those who have turned their grievance into gunpowder, their ideology into shrapnel. To speak of their fate is to trace a line through the ledgers of federal justice, where the ledger entries are measured not in dollars, but in decades, in lifetimes, and occasionally, in the final, sterile stillness of a needle.

Consider, if you will, the spectrum of their ends. It is a history written in the ink of maximum security and the cold arithmetic of the sentencing guidelines.

THE ARCHITECT OF THE HEARTLAND'S SORROW: TIMOTHY MCVEIGH

At the pinnacle of this grim roster stands Timothy McVeigh, the young man with the hard, flat eyes who brought the Federal Building in Oklahoma City to its knees in April 1995. His crime was a thunderclap in the heart of the nation, a massacre of innocence that demanded a reckoning of biblical proportion. The justice meted out to him was swift and absolute. He was not destined for the long, gray twilight of a prison cell. Instead, the federal government, with a steadiness that matched his own calculated fury, sought and secured the ultimate sanction. In June of 2001, McVeigh was strapped to a gurney in Terre Haute, Indiana and executed by lethal injection, the first federal prisoner to be put to death in nearly 40 years. His sentence was a message, stark and unadorned: for the architect of such devastation: there is no room left in the world of the living.

THE SILENT ACCOMPLICE: TERRY NICHOLS

Then there is Terry Nichols, the shadow to McVeigh's lightning. His hands were stained with the same ammonium nitrate, his mind clouded by the same anti-government fever. But his fate was different. The jury, perhaps seeing a distinction between the mastermind and the mechanic, or perhaps simply weary of death, spared him the executioner's needle. Instead, they handed him a life, or rather, 161 of them. He resides now in the concrete womb of ADX Florence in Fremont County, Colorado, the "Alcatraz of the Rockies," sentenced to life without the possibility of parole—a ghost in a supermax machine, condemned to wither away in a silence as profound as the grave.

THE HERMIT OF THE WOODS:
TED KACZYNSKI

And what of the Unabomber? Theodore Kaczynski, that brilliant, twisted mathematician who waged a lonely war against modernity from a shack in Montana. For nearly 20 years, he mailed death in brown paper packages, a phantom haunting the U.S. Postal Service. When the law finally pried him from his wilderness, the outcome was a foregone conclusion of sorts. To avoid the death penalty, he bartered his life. He pleaded guilty, accepting eight consecutive life sentences without the possibility of parole. Like Nichols, he was swallowed by ADX Florence, a brilliant mind left to decay in a concrete box until his death by suicide in 2023—a quiet, solitary end to a loud and violent life.

THE WANDERING BOMBER:
ERIC RUDOLPH

Eric Rudolph, the man who planted bombs at abortion clinics and the Atlanta Olympics, spent years as a specter in the Appalachian mist. When he was finally captured, scavenging for food like a feral animal, he, too, struck a deal with the devil he despised—the federal government. To save his own skin, to avoid the lethal injection, he revealed the locations of his hidden explosives. The price was four consecutive life sentences. He remains buried in the same supermax tomb as the others, a man who once sought to be a soldier of God now reduced to a prisoner of the Bureau of Prisons.

THE NEW FACE OF HATE:
DYLANN ROOF AND BEYOND

The ledger continues, updated by a new generation of hate. Dylann Roof, a young man with a bowl cut and a heart full of racial poison, slaughtered worshippers in a Charleston, South Carolina church in 2015. For him, there was no mercy, no deal. The federal jury, looking into the abyss of his crimes, returned a sentence of death. He sits now on death row at USP Terre Haute in Vigo County, Indiana, waiting for a date that will close his chapter.

And others follow, a parade of lost souls. Robert Gregory Bowers, the Pittsburgh synagogue shooter, sentenced to death. Patrick Crusius, the Walmart shooter in El Paso, handed 90 consecutive life sentences. Payton Gendron, the Buffalo supermarket shooter, given life without parole.

In this country, the sentencing of a domestic terrorist is rarely a simple affair. It is a theater of high stakes, where the death penalty hangs like a Sword of Damocles, often traded away for a lifetime of concrete and steel. The outcome, invariably, is removal—a surgical excision of the offender from the body politic, leaving them to exist only as a name in a file, a cautionary tale whispered in the dark.

THE LONG WAIT

In the sterile, fluorescent-washed corridors of SCI Phoenix, time does not march; it merely pools, stagnant and gray. As of this New Year's Day in 2026, Eric Matthew Frein sits within a climate of exquisite legal suspension, a man who has been weighed by the scales of justice and found heavy enough for the grave, yet who remains stubbornly above it. He is a resident of that most peculiar of American zip codes: the Pennsylvania death row, a place where the law's ultimate finality has been quietly arrested by the stroke of a governor's pen.

The machinery of his undoing, once so loud and relentless, has subsided into the hushed, paper-shuffling labor of the post-conviction relief act. The high courts have already had their say; the Pennsylvania Supreme Court, in that distant spring of 2019, gazed upon the evidence—the journals, the blood-stained asphalt, the cold geometry of the sniper's nest—and affirmed that the State indeed possessed the right to extinguish his life. By early 2020, the highest court in the land turned its face away, refusing to hear his pleas, and for a brief, breathless moment, it seemed the ledger would be closed.

But in the Commonwealth, the shadow of the gallows is long and curiously thin. Governor Shapiro, following the path of his predecessor, has maintained a moratorium that acts as a silencer upon the executioner's rifle. Death warrants are signed with a grim regularity, only to be met with reprieves that carry the weight of a permanent stay. Frein exists now in a state of "protracted waiting," a condition where the cell has widened slightly—granting him those few dozen hours of communal air—but the horizon remains a wall of stone.

His lawyers continue to toil in the subterranean levels of the appellate process, weaving a tapestry of "mitigating circumstances" and "procedural errors" that the jury in Pike County once so decisively shredded. They speak of damaged brains and parental shadows, trying to find a crack in the verdict through which mercy might leak. Yet, while the lawyers argue and the reprieves accumulate, the families in Blooming Grove carry a different kind of sentence—one that does not offer the luxury of a stay. For Frein, the law has become a labyrinth of his own making, a ghost in a machine that refuses to either kill him or set him free.

THE PROSECUTOR'S TAKE

The Pike County Courthouse in Milford had been restored to its ordinary quiet. Yet, within the functional, fluorescent calm of District Attorney Ray Tonkin's office, the drama of the Frein prosecution persisted, meticulously filed and cataloged. Tonkin himself was the unblinking, necessary functionary of the State, a man who measured his moral landscape in evidence and statutes.

He was also a man of measured words, carefully crafted to protect his ongoing efforts to see that the courtroom victory, if you could call it that, was preserved.

When I settled across from the meticulously dressed DA, I sought to engage not the prosecutor, but the conscience. I began, then, at the abyss: the decision to seek the death penalty.

"It did not conflict with any of my beliefs," Tonkin stated, his voice carrying the deep, resonant certainty of a man who rarely permits personal conflicts to blur professional duty. "I believe in the death penalty. In this instance, I believe the death penalty was deserved."

It was a cold, absolute statement. Frein's crime—that calculated ambush on a September night—had earned the ultimate currency of the State's wrath.

The evidence in *Commonwealth v. Frein* had been vast, a relentless torrent of science, digital footprints, and the killer's own damning words. An embarrassment of proof, really, a mountain that one might, in a less consequential case, risk appearing as "piling on."

I asked how one manages such an excess of proof without risking the appearance of overwhelming the defense. Tonkin shrugged, the gesture dismissing the notion of excess.

"No. Because of the penalty that was being sought. A jury deserves to know the evidence that's there."

He introduced then the philosophical conundrum that haunts the jury room in a capital case: the specter of residual doubt.

"Jurors may be of the opinion that somebody is guilty beyond a reasonable doubt," he explained, "and even though that's the standard for guilt... the jurors want something to be in their own mind beyond all doubt."

Tonkin knew that even after the legal standard is met, the human conscience, when asked to order an execution, demands an absolute, moral certainty. His objective, therefore, was not merely to prove guilt, but to surgically obliterate every lingering shadow. For that, he relied on the irrefutable.

"The strongest piece of evidence was the direct connection between the firearm used to assassinate Corporal Brian Dickson and severely wound Trooper Alex Douglass... and it was found with him, with his DNA on it."

The ballistics, the genetic signature, the unassailable truth of the science—that was the hammer that drove the verdict home.

Frein, even in his confession, had elevated his crime by using a specific, weighted word. He called it an "assassination." I asked Tonkin about the significance of that term, and whether he viewed the defendant as a domestic terrorist.

"I think he was convicted of terrorism. So I think he is a convicted terrorist."

He drew the distinction between a private act of malice and a public assault on the fabric of the state, rooting his belief in the symbolic choice of the target:

"A uniformed police officer is perhaps the most visible form of government... Based on [Frein's] writings and what he wanted to try to do and to effectuate change, I think it was purposeful to go after a uniformed police officer because they are the most visible form of government in our society."

It was a cold, precise statement of strategy. Frein was not aiming at an individual, but at the symbol—the most accessible and recognizable agent of the authority he despised. He pointed out the crucial, chilling fact that a civilian dispatcher had left the barracks door shortly before the first shot, and Frein had ignored her. "It was purposeful to go after a uniformed police officer," he concluded.

The current political reality in Pennsylvania—the gubernatorial moratorium on executions—had seemingly rendered the death sentence itself academic. But Tonkin, a functionary of process, was untouched by this temporary stasis.

"The moratorium has no impact on this case yet because it hasn't been through the litigation stages to get to that point where a governor could decide to grant a reprieve."

His concern, the only concern permissible in his role, was the immediate legal future: the post-conviction litigation. This is where the defense, having failed to save Frein's life, attempts to preserve it.

He dismissed the defense's primary narrative—the "broken boy" who was a product of abuse—as ineffective, not necessarily for a lack of sympathy, but for a lack of proof.

"The jury found that there were aggravating factors and no mitigating factors... You know, all twelve jurors did decide that none of the mitigating factors that they put forth were proven by a preponderance of the evidence."

The defense's strategy failed because they could not meet the legal standard of proof necessary to activate the jury's mercy.

We spoke of Frein's chilling demeanor during his confession, the casual coffee and cigar, and the defense's subsequent attempt to portray their client as a "broken boy." Tonkin countered this with an example of the defense's expert testimony, which sought to paint prison life as a crushing, dehumanizing punishment.

"It's kind of like the old story of Br'er Rabbit, you know? 'Oh, please don't throw me in that briar patch.' Trying to say that briar patch is so bad, don't throw me in it... It's kind of a trick on the jurors, in my view."

This, the suggestion that imprisonment was a fate worse than death, was an artifice Tonkin sought to dismantle, using his own experts to assure the jury that life on death row was not a continual torment. "Prison is the punishment," he stated. "It is not a place where people go to be punished." He believed the defense's strategy—the "broken boy" narrative and the manufactured fear of imprisonment—was wholly unpersuasive.

While Tonkin was not in charge of the manhunt itself, he was keenly aware of the psychological weight it placed on the community he was sworn to protect.

"I had a grave concern that he was going to hurt another individual or individuals," he admitted. "And I had a concern that he would be apprehended without further injury to anyone."

The deployment of IEDs (improvised explosive devices), discovered by the police, amplified that fear from a simple manhunt into a crisis of public safety. The anxiety felt by residents—afraid to take out their trash at night—was a constant pressure, a variable that required him to prepare his case in the midst of a terrifying, ongoing emergency.

We spoke of the publicity that necessitated the jury being pulled from outside the local coverage area, a logistical hurdle that forced Tonkin to study the people of Chester County.

"I had to find out about... the people of Chester County... and what I found out was, there were a large number of people there, that were willing to set aside their personal business... and hear this case."

He drew an interesting comparison: "I believe in a great parallel between military service and juror service. They're really the only two acts that are compulsory as citizens, in America." To this writer, reflecting on his own service said it was an honor, an obligation, a unique compulsory service to the greater good.

Finally, I asked the ultimate question: Was Frein truly evil?

Having served as a police officer and now as a prosecutor, Tonkin did not equivocate. "Many people in society, in order for their own mental self-preservation... want to label issues with people like this as mental health issues when it's really an evil issue... I just believe that there's evil in this world."

Did Frein, with his mundane life and his singular act of malice, fit that description?

"Yes," Tonkin confirmed. "I believe he represents true evil."

The assessment, delivered with Tonkin's customary precision, was the final word from the man whose duty it was to deliver the ultimate penalty. The man who sought to tear down the government with two rifle shots is now subject entirely to its mechanisms. Tonkin, the architect of that process, is ready to continue the long, meticulous wait.

EPILOGUE

It was a thing to be considered, this shattering. One thought of the bullet itself, a small, cold, hard thing of lead, traveling at an inconceivable velocity. It was a fragment, really, but one with the power to tear a great hole in the fabric of things.

First, there was the trooper, Corporal Bryon Dickson. He was a man with a wife, a life, a future, all of it held together by the ordinary, unremarkable routines of his days. A husband, a father, a son. Then came the bullet, and in its passing, it tore all of that away, leaving behind a silence and an absence that would be forever filled with grief.

There was Trooper Alex Douglass. His life, too, was forever changed in that same instant. The bullet struck him, not with finality, but with a different sort of permanence. He would live, yes, but forever after, he would carry the memory of the cold earth and the shattered flesh. He was a man marked, a testament to the night's violence.

And then there were the families. The Dicksons, who would never again hear the sound of Bryon's voice. The Douglasses, who would watch a loved one struggle and mend, but never fully recover. The circle of their lives, once whole, was now irrevocably broken.

Finally, there were the Freins, the family of the perpetrator. Their life, too, was a casualty, though in a different way.

Theirs was a private sort of pain, a quiet devastation that came not from a bullet, but from a truth: that their son, their brother, had become something monstrous, a thing of infamy. Theirs was a tragedy of association, a life lived forever in the cold shadow of a terrible and incomprehensible act.

ACKNOWLEDGMENTS

Writing is a solitary pursuit, but it is never a solo effort. I owe a debt of gratitude to those who helped bring this book to life.

My deepest thanks go to my son, Austin Hicks-Frank. His unwavering support and honest critiques were invaluable, pushing me to be a better writer. He is my first and most important audience.

I am also profoundly grateful to my longtime colleague, Chris Mele, who saw the potential in this project from the very beginning. His single piece of advice after reviewing an early draft—"slow it down"—was a pivotal turning point, forcing me to step back and craft a more deliberate and compelling narrative.

Pike County District Attorney Ray Tonkin, who successfully prosecuted the case, was generous with his time and insights that added texture and context to the story.

A debt of gratitude goes out to my literary agent, Anne G. Devlin of the Max Gartenberg Literary Agency, for her encouragement, support, keen advice, and believing in me. And thanks to Kevin Thomas, Ed Eccker, and Damon Bee for their contributions to this project.

I would also like to thank my longtime brother-in-arms, Tommy Shaw, whose constant encouragement helped propel me forward in this project.

Finally, I want to express my gratitude to all my friends as well as my colleagues at HORIBA, who patiently endured my endless lunchtime "fact-dumping" sessions. Your willingness to listen and engage helped me sort through the vast amount of research and identify the most crucial details of this tragic story.

MOTHERS AND MURDERERS
BY KATHERINE ELLISON

https://wbp.bz/mothersmurderersa